THE MASTERY OF SELF

THE MASTERY OF SELF

A TOLTEC GUIDE TO PERSONAL FREEDOM

❖

DON MIGUEL RUIZ JR.

Hier⊙phant publishing

Cover design by Emma Smith
Cover art © Nicholas Wilton | Illustration Source
Interior by Frame25 Productions

Hierophant Publishing
San Antonio, TX

www.hierophantpublishing.com

If you are unable to order this book from your local bookseller,
you may order directly from the publisher.

Library of Congress Cataloging in Publication data has been
applied for.

ISBN: 978-1-938289-69-9

17 16 15

To all whom I love.

Contents

A Message from the Publisher:
How This Book Came into Being   xi

Explanation of Key Terms   xv

Introduction   xix

1. The Making of a Master   1

2. Understanding Our
Domestication and Attachments   9

3. Unconditional Love for Yourself   31

4. Unconditional Love for Others   49

5. Spotting the Triggers
and Maneuvering the Traps   69

6. Breaking the Cycle of the Automatic   91

7. Multiple Masks   107

8. Goal Setting   123

9. Comparison and Competition   139

My Wish for You   155

Acknowledgments   163

A Message from the Publisher: How This Book Came into Being

Know Thyself

These were the words inscribed at the entrance of the Temple of Apollo, home of the Oracle of Delphi, arguably the most famous woman in all of Ancient Greece. History tells us that thousands upon thousands of people, including kings, queens, statesmen, philosophers, and common people alike, would travel hundreds of miles or more to receive her prophetic guidance every year. The temple itself was a towering structure that reached its pinnacle of influence in the middle centuries of the first millennia BCE. At the time, it was considered the most important religious shrine in all of Greece.

Building a massive temple like this, even with our advanced machinery and modern technology, would still be a major undertaking by today's standards. Modern architects marvel at the intelligence, craftsmanship, and labor that went into creating this temple, but I find it more fascinating that of all the messages that could have been written at its entrance, the two-word axiom "Know Thyself" was chosen. Perhaps the oracle wanted to be sure that if you remembered only one message from your pilgrimage, then knowing yourself should be it. I often wonder what the world would look like today if some of our modern religions taught that self-knowledge, rather than blind adherence to external guidance and dogma, was the paramount goal of the spiritual path.

Not long after the zenith of the oracle, and on the other side of the world, a group of people came together to form a new civilization in what is now south central Mexico. They called themselves Toltec, which means "artist." But these people were not artists in the traditional sense (although some were painters and sculptors also); rather, they saw themselves as artists of life, and the world we inhabit as the canvas upon which they painted their masterpiece. The legacy of the Toltecs and their teachings has been handed down from generation to generation, often in secrecy when the politics of the day required it, and don Miguel Ruiz Jr. is the latest teacher in the Eagle Knight lineage of the Toltec people.

When Miguel approached me about writing a book on self-mastery, I couldn't help but think of the Oracle of Delphi and her 2,500-year-old instruction to Know Thyself. I wondered how this sage advice would appear in the context of his Toltec ancestry. The book you are holding now, I am pleased to say, conveys exactly this—and much, much more. Miguel presents ancient wisdom in a modern way, and helps us to apply this timeless truth of Know Thyself in our everyday lives.

In the opening chapters, Miguel lays the groundwork for the book, providing a framework based on his Toltec tradition. He explains how the events and actions of your past have shaped your present reality. The following chapters are where he really digs in, giving you the tools you need to discover who you are at the deepest level, uncover any self-limiting beliefs you have falsely accepted as fact, and release any attachments you are holding that continuously drag you down. The later chapters will help you chart a new course to where you really want to go, which for some of you may be a very different place than where you are currently heading.

Miguel has stressed to me on many occasions that it's not enough to just read the information contained in these pages; it's when you choose to incorporate this knowledge into your life that you receive the benefits.

To this aim, he has included exercises at the end of many chapters that are designed to help you do just that. Returning to the Greek world for a moment, we can say that the exercises are where *logos* (knowledge) becomes *praxis* (practice)—or, as Miguel writes, "understanding the teachings is the first step, but applying them is what makes you a Master."

So without further ado, it is with great pleasure that I present to you don Miguel Ruiz Jr.'s *The Mastery of Self*. May it serve you well on your journey of self-discovery.

Randy Davila
Publisher
Hierophant Publishing

Explanation of Key Terms

Ally—The voice of your internal narrator when it inspires you to live, create, and love unconditionally. The ally can also offer constructive self-talk.

Attachment—The action of taking something that is not a part of you and making it a part of you through an emotional or energetic investment. You can attach to external objects, beliefs, ideas, and even roles you play in the world.

Authentic Self—The Divine inside of you; the force that gives life to your mind and your body. It's similar to the concept of the spirit or the soul that is present in many religious traditions, but it's not exactly the same.

Awareness—The practice of paying attention in the present moment to what is happening inside your body and your mind as well as in your immediate surroundings.

Domestication—The primary system of control in the Dream of the Planet. Starting when we are very young, we are presented with either a reward or a punishment for adopting the beliefs and behaviors of what others find acceptable. When we adopt these beliefs and behaviors as a result of either the reward or punishment, we can say we have been domesticated.

Dream of the Planet—The combination of every single being in the world's Personal Dream, or the world we live in.

Narrators—The voices in your mind that speak to you throughout the day, which can be either positive (ally) or negative (parasite).

Parasite—The voice of the narrator when it uses your beliefs, formed through domestication and attachment, to hold power over you by placing conditions on your self-love and self-acceptance. This negative voice causes sadness, anxiety, and fear.

Personal Dream—The unique reality created by every individual; your personal perspective. It is the manifestation of the relationship between your mind and body.

Toltec people—An ancient group of Native Americans who came together in south and central Mexico to study perception. The word *Toltec* means "artist."

Toltec warrior—One who is committed to using the teachings of the Toltec tradition to win the inner battle against domestication and attachment.

Introduction

IMAGE FOR A MOMENT that you are in a dream.

In this dream, you find yourself at a huge party with thousands of people, where you are the only sober person and everyone else is drunk. The other partygoers are in varying states of intoxication. A few people have had just one or two drinks and are only tipsy; most fall into the realm of general drunkenness; and a handful are so drunk that they are making spectacles of themselves in all sorts of colorful ways. They may even have blacked out, as their actions seem completely out of their control.

Some of the people at this party are your friends and family, some are acquaintances, but most you don't know. You try to talk to a few people, but you quickly realize that their intoxication level has altered their ability to communicate clearly; it has clouded their viewpoint. You also notice that each person is experiencing the party differently, depending on his or her degree of drunkenness, and your interactions change with every drink they consume.

The partygoers range from loud, outgoing, and merry, to shy, quiet, and sullen. As the party rages on, you watch everyone alternate between the two ends of the spectrum: from happy to sad, excited to apathetic. They fight and make up, argue, embrace, and argue again, and you watch as this type of odd behavior repeats itself endlessly in cycles throughout the night. You realize that even though they are drunk, it's not the booze they crave more of, but rather the drama of the party.

As the night continues, your interactions with the partygoers vary from person to person. While some are enjoyable, others have the potential to quickly turn volatile. Since their perception is clouded, the other partygoers react emotionally to situations that you can see are pure fantasy. For some of them, the dream has become a nightmare.

Most important of all, it's clear that no one at this party knows this is all just a dream.

Then it occurs to you that this is not a new party, but one you've attended before. At one point you were just like them. You went through all the varying degrees of drunkenness, behaving exactly as those around you are now. You conversed through the fog of booze, joined the folly of the party, and let the intoxication guide your actions.

Finally, it's clear that no one there realizes you are now sober. They think you are still drunk, just like them. They do not see your path, only their own. They view you only as a distortion, projected by their alcohol-addled minds, not as you actually are. They are also completely unaware of the true effect the liquor is having on them. Each is lost in his or her own dream of the party. They do not see how their interactions are no longer under their control. As a result, they continually try to entice you to join the drama of the party, to join the folly that their distorted perception has created.

What will you do?

Chapter One

The Making of a Master

AT THE PEAK OF her journey, a Toltec warrior clears her mind of beliefs, domestication, and attachments, marking the end of a war within herself for personal freedom. Surrounding her is an infinite number of possibilities, each one a choice that leads in a unique direction in life. When she makes a choice through her action, she knows that the path she follows is ultimately no different than the other paths, as they all lead to the same place. She has no demands for any outcome, as she realizes that there is nowhere she needs to go and nothing she needs to do in order to find herself. Her action is a result of the pure joy of realizing that she is alive at this moment to choose one of the many possibilities.

This living with a quiet mind creates a state of pure bliss that comes from being entirely in the moment. Truly nothing matters but the present, because it is the only place where life can express itself.

This is a state that many of you have experienced at some point in your life, when you were completely engaged in the now. Some people experience it while they are exercising, consciously creating, being in nature, making love, or, of course, meditating or praying. It's the moment when the mind and the body are in complete awareness of the experience of life. It can also be said that it is during these moments that we often reach a pure state of unconditional love for everything and everyone, including ourselves.

While living full-time in this state of pure bliss is a goal for many, most will agree it is easier said than done— especially if we don't live isolated away from the world. Surrounded by other people, we choose who we will interact and engage with, and it's often in these interactions that the trouble begins.

In the Toltec tradition, the main function of the mind is to dream, or to perceive and to project information. The Personal Dream is the unique reality created by every individual; it's their perspective, a manifestation of the relationship between mind and body, and intent is the energy that animates both. As our shared knowledge and experience mingle together, we co-create the Dream of the Planet, which is the combination of every single being in the world's Personal Dream. While we live individual dreams based on our individual perceptions, the Dream of the Planet is the manifestation of our shared intentions, where we allow our ideas and agreements to flow between us. If there is harmony in the Personal Dream, then there is a constant opportunity for harmony with the Dream of the Planet.

Since you are reading this book, it's likely that you don't live in a cloistered monastery or ashram, or all alone high atop a mountain. You have chosen to engage in the world, and you want to enjoy yourself in the process. Solitude can be a great tool for healing and communion with oneself, but it is our interactions with others that will allow us to thrive and enjoy an active life. If life is like a carnival, you have come to ride the rides.

But engaging in the Dream means you will likely develop preferences for certain potential paths—or, in other words, you will have wants and desires. When you become too attached to those desires and they aren't fulfilled, the result is that you suffer. There are also billions of others involved in co-creating the Dream of the Planet, many of whom have wants and desires that are different from yours. Without respect and understanding, drama, disagreement, and even conflict are sure to occur. This begs the question, is there a way you can engage in an active life without becoming too attached to your own personal preferences? Can you remain calm and balanced when dealing with others, seeing them and yourself through the eyes of unconditional love, and consequently not be drawn into the drama of the party? In my experience the answer to both questions is yes, and that is the subject of this book. This can be done through a process called the Mastery of Self.

You become a Master of Self when you can engage the Dream of the Planet and everyone in it without losing sight of your Authentic Self, and while maintaining the awareness that every choice you make is your own. You are no longer caught up in the drama of the party. When you engage with the Dream of the Planet with the awareness and remembrance that it's only a dream, you are able to move freely, liberated from the chains of attachment and domestication.

An attachment is the action of taking something that is not a part of you and making it a part of you through an emotional or energetic investment. When you become attached to something in the Dream of the Planet, you suffer every time the object of your attachment is threatened, and this is true regardless of if the threat is real or an illusion. Most people not only attach to their wants and desires as they relate to material things, but also to their beliefs and ideas. Although an attachment is something that can occur naturally in the moment, it becomes unhealthy when you lose the ability to detach from it when the moment ends or when the belief no longer reflects the truth. In many ways, attachments to beliefs are far more destructive than attachments to external items, because beliefs and ideas are much harder to spot and let go of.

Domestication is the system of control in the Dream of the Planet; it is the way we learn conditional love. Starting when we are very young, we are presented with either a reward or a punishment for adopting the beliefs and behaviors of others in the Dream. This system of reward and punishment, or domestication, is used to control our behavior. The result of domestication is that many of us give up who we really are in exchange for who we think we should be, and consequently we end up living a life that is not our own. Learning how to spot and release our domestication, and reclaiming who we really are in the process, is a hallmark of a Master of Self.

When you become so domesticated by or attached to a belief or idea that you can't let go of it, your choices narrow until any notion of choice is really an illusion. Your beliefs now define you, and they will dictate your choice. You are no longer the master of your own self, as your domestication and attachments are controlling you. As a result, you will engage with others and yourself in a way that does not serve your highest good. You have joined into the drama of the party, and it now shapes your Personal Dream.

The Dream of the Planet is full of traps to lure you back into the drama of the party, and falling into one of them can happen in the blink of an eye. If you choose to engage with the world, avoiding all traps is virtually impossible. However, when you become aware that you are falling into a trap, the simple act of noticing it allows you to begin to regain control. As you get better at spotting the traps and understanding your own underlying emotions and beliefs that make them traps for you in the first place, you are far less likely to take the bait. And even when you do, you can let go of whatever you are attached too as quickly as your will dictates. It may seem counterintuitive, but *you choose to let go in order to be in control.* Doing so is the Mastery of Self in action.

As a Master of Self, you can have relationships with others, even those who disagree with you, while still being grounded in your Authentic Self. You are able to maintain your free will and respect the free will of others. Knowing that others see you in a specific way gives you choices when you engage with them. You shape-shift only in their perception, and your awareness of that allows you to stay true to yourself and not give in to the temptation to take on others' definitions of who you are. You realize that you don't have to put on any image that others project onto you because you know it is not your reality. With this awareness, you will be better able to co-create harmoniously with others, making the relationships that matter most to you more fulfilling and rewarding.

Most importantly, when you become a Master of Self, you know how to stay grounded in your Authentic Self regardless of what's happening around you. You also have the awareness to realize quickly when you are acting in a way that isn't helpful to yourself or others and can spot those situations when you are feeding your ego, or the false sense of self, instead of living in peace. In this way, you free yourself from the drama and self-inflicted suffering created by so many people.

Without awareness of how to engage the Dream of the Planet and the beings who create it, it is too easy to internalize what is happening around you, or to forget that it is all a dream. As a result, your attachments grow until you are consumed with the drama of the party. Becoming a Master of Self is about maintaining awareness of your center while you are interacting with the Dream of the Planet, remembering that it's all a dream. Staying centered while engaging with the world is much easier said than done, and this book will be devoted to teaching you exactly how to do that.

Self-mastery is not an isolated idea within the Toltec tradition, as every form of spiritual discipline provides a map to help us live in harmony within the Dream of the Planet by freeing our mind from the tyranny of our own thinking and being affected by the projections of others. That being said, the Toltec tradition has some unique contributions to this effort, and we'll discuss these in greater detail in the pages that follow.

Before we deconstruct and rebuild the world around us, starting with ourselves, we need a greater understanding of attachments, domestication, and the difference between conditional and unconditional love. Then, and only then, can we reconstruct our Personal Dream in peace and harmony.

Chapter Two

Understanding Our
Domestication and Attachments

THERE IS AN OLD Toltec story that has been shared across generations in my family about a shaman who called himself the Smokey Mirror. He gave himself this name once he became aware of the smoke that not only clouded his vision and controlled his will, but also did the same to everyone around him. A recounting of the Smokey Mirror story will be helpful as we begin to go deeper into the Mastery of Self.

After many years of study and in a moment of great realization, a shaman experiences the truth. "I am made of light; I am made of stars. The real us is pure love, pure light," he says. As he looks around his village, he knows that everyone and everything he sees is a manifestation of God, and he intuitively understands that the human journey is a process of the Divine becoming aware of Itself.

Moved by this realization, the shaman immediately wants to share this information with everyone in his village. But when he does so, it becomes clear to him that no one else understands. The shaman then realizes that there is a smoky fog between him and others, and this fog doesn't allow people to see beyond the tip of their own nose. The fog controls their every action, every belief.

The shaman also notices that as he interacts with others the fog tries to assert its control over him again. But as soon as he notices the fog creeping back in, the simple act of noticing makes the fog dissipate. As the fog recedes, he becomes aware of a mirror in front of him and he can vaguely see his reflection. When the fog completely clears, he can see himself fully again.

The shaman is aware that he is the truth, and the reflection in the mirror is a reminder; it only reflects the truth. He begins to understand the reflection as an instrument of awareness.

Every time the fog begins to creep in and keep him from knowing who he really is, he can look to his mirror.

If it is cloudy or he can't see himself, he knows he is on the wrong track, trapped in the fog. But as soon as he remembers his Authentic Self, the smoke immediately begins to clear. To remind himself of who he really is and the power of the fog to obscure his perception, the shaman changes his name to the Smokey Mirror.

This powerful story encapsulates a core teaching in my family's Toltec tradition. The fog represents our attachments and our domestications, which together keep us from experiencing the truth of who we are.

Domestication

Let me begin to explain domestication with a simple story.

Imagine a child of eight or nine having lunch with his grandmother, who has prepared soup for their afternoon meal. They sit together and converse, enjoying each other's company and the love they share.

After finishing half his bowl of soup, the child realizes he is full. "I don't want the rest, Grandmother. I am full."

"You must eat all your soup, Grandson," she replies.

Whether you are a parent or not, it is likely clear what this boy's grandmother is trying to do. Her intentions are admirable; she wants him to eat in order to be nourished. When he declines, she tries to convince him to eat more by offering him a reward for doing what she wants. This is the first tool of domestication.

"You must finish your soup," she says. "It will make you grow up big and strong, like Superman!"

But the young boy is undeterred. "No, I am not hungry," he insists. "I don't want to eat any more right now."

In addition to not being hungry, the child is also enjoying the feeling of asserting himself, because it feels powerful to say no, to express his free will. He can also feel that same sense of power when he says yes to the things he wants, and it feels good to say it. This is how young children (including ourselves when we were young) learn about the power of intent: by stating yes and no.

Eventually, the boy reaches the threshold of his grandmother's patience, and when the carrot doesn't work, she reaches for the stick to impose her will upon him. Like many grandparents and their parents before them, she crosses the line of respect for his choice and adds punishment—in this case, guilt and shaming, which is the second tool of domestication.

"Do you know how many children don't have anything to eat around the world? They are starving! And here you are, wasting your food. It's a sin to waste food!"

Now the young boy is concerned. He doesn't want to look like a selfish child, and he really doesn't want to be seen as a sinner in his grandmother's eyes. With a sense of defeat, he relents and subjugates his will.

"OK, Grandma, I will finish my soup."

He begins to eat again, and he doesn't stop until the bowl is empty. Then, with the tenderness that makes her grandson feel safe and loved, Grandma says, "That's my good boy."

The boy learns that by complying with the rules of the dream, he can earn a reward; in this case, he is a good boy in the eyes of his grandmother and receives her love and encouragement. The punishment would have been to be seen as a selfish child, a sinner in her eyes, and a bad boy.

This is a simple example of domestication in action. No one doubts that the grandmother has the best of intentions; she loves her grandson and wants him to eat his lunch, but the method she is using to achieve that goal has negative unintended consequences. Anytime guilt and shame are deployed as tools to provoke action, this counters any good that has been achieved. Eventually, these negative elements will resurface in one way or another.

In this case, let's imagine that when this boy grows up, the domestication that occurred around this issue is so strong that it still has an imposing power over him well into adulthood. For instance, many years later he goes into a restaurant where they serve a big plate of food, and halfway through his meal his body signals to him the truth of that moment: *I am full.*

Consciously, or subconsciously, he hears a voice: *It's a sin to waste food.*

Consciously, or subconsciously, he answers *Yes, Grandma,* and continues to eat.

Finishing his plate like a good boy, he responds to his domestication rather than his needs of the moment. In that instant, he completely goes against himself by continuing to eat after his body has already let him know that he is full. The idea is so strong that it overrules his body's natural preference to stop. Overeating may damage his body, which is one of the negative consequences in this case of using guilt and shame as a tool. The other consequence is that he is experiencing internal suffering by reliving a past moment of guilt and shame, and it is controlling his actions in the present.

Finally, note that his grandmother is not even present in the current situation, as he has now taken up the reins of domestication and subjugated his own will without anyone's else's influence. In the Toltec tradition we refer to this phenomenon as self-domestication. As my father likes to say, "Humans are the only animals on the planet that self-domesticate."

The relationship between the boy and his grandmother forms a part of the Dream of the Planet, and the lunch between the grandmother and her grandson is a basic example of how domestication and self-domestication within the Dream occurs. The grandmother domesticated her grandson in that moment, but he continued to self-domesticate himself long after that. Self-domestication is the act of accepting ourselves on the condition that we live up to the ideals we have adopted from others in the Dream of the Planet, without ever considering if those ideals are what we truly want.

While the consequences of finishing a bowl of soup are minimal, domestication and self-domestication can take much more serious and darker forms as well. For instance, many of us learned to be critical of our physical appearance because it wasn't "good enough" by society's standards. We were presented with the belief that we weren't tall enough, thin enough, or that our skin wasn't the right color, and the moment we agreed with that belief we began to self-domesticate. Because we adopted an external belief, we either rejected or tried to change our physical appearance so we could feel worthy of our own self-acceptance and the acceptance of others. Imagine for a moment the many industries that would cease to exist if we all loved our bodies exactly the way they are.

To be clear, domestication regarding body image is different from wanting to lose weight in order to be healthy, or even having a preference to look a certain way. The key difference is that with a preference, you come from a place of self-love and self-acceptance, whereas with domestication you start from a place of shame, guilt, and not being "enough." The line between these two can be thin sometimes, and a Master of Self is one who can look within and determine his or her true motive.

Another popular form of domestication in the current Dream of the Planet revolves around social class and material possessions. There is an underlying belief promulgated by society that those who have the most "stuff" or who hold certain jobs are somehow more important than the rest. I, for one, have never met anyone who was more important than anyone else, as we are all beautiful and unique creations of the Divine. And yet many people pursue career paths they dislike and buy things they don't really want or need all in an effort to achieve the elusive goals of peer acceptance and self-acceptance. Instances such as these (and we can think of many others) are the ways in which domestication leads to self-domestication, and the result is that we have people living lives that aren't their own.

Let me share an example of a close friend who was domesticated in this way, and how he broke free. From a very young age, my friend was encouraged by his family to become a lawyer. They filled his young mind with stories of money and power, and told him he had all the skills necessary to be successful in this endeavor. With the encouragement of his family, my friend studied pre-law in college and then went straight into law school. But shortly after he arrived, he found that he couldn't stand the practice of law. In hindsight, he realized he had been domesticated to the idea that being an attorney was going to make him rich, powerful, and, most importantly, special in the eyes of his family, but the truth was that in adopting this path he was following their dreams instead of his own. When he announced to his family that he was dropping out of law school, many of them were disappointed and tried desperately to change his mind, but he was able to stay firm by relying on his own intent. That was many years ago, and he now chuckles when he remembers his former plans, as he is very happy in his current profession as an author and spiritual teacher.

This example illustrates how ideas that were planted in us as children and beyond often don't reflect our preferred path. But, just like my friend, you have the power inside you to break free from any domestication that you've experienced, and the first step to doing so is becoming aware of that domestication and finding out what is true for you.

Lastly, I want to be clear that although I have been focused on the negative aspects of domestication, not all domestication results in negative consequences. In other words, just because an idea was planted in you via domestication doesn't mean that the idea is a bad one and you must reject it. If it is consistent with your true preferences in life, that's wonderful. For instance, if my friend had ended up enjoying the practice of law, then there would have been no reason to make a career change. Once you decide for yourself with a clear mind that a particular idea or belief works for you, there's nothing wrong with maintaining it. The point is that you make a conscious choice.

Attachment

In its most basic sense, attachment begins with items in the world. You can see this in young children, around the age of two, when they first begin to associate and declare objects in their possession as "mine." Anyone who has ever attempted to make a two-year-old part with a toy can attest to the power of attachment. Although this is where attachment to items begins, it certainly doesn't end there, as often the more harmful attachments we hold are the unseen ones, and by this I mean our attachment to our own ideas, opinions, and beliefs.

In my previous book, *The Five Levels of Attachment*, I explain the concept of attachment in detail, and I offer a measuring stick for the varying degrees to which you can become tied to your own beliefs, ideas, and opinions. For the purposes of understanding attachment and how it relates to the Mastery of Self, I will use an abbreviated example of a popular story that appears in that book. This example illustrates how if we aren't careful, attachments can quickly become unhealthy and cause suffering in our lives.

Imagine that you like soccer. You don't have a particular team or player that you root for, and it doesn't matter if it's taking place in a magnificent stadium or a dirt-filled field; both are equally good for a fan who just loves watching the game. The players could be great or mediocre and you wouldn't care, as long as everyone playing is enjoying the game. As you watch, you generally don't choose to root for or against one side, and even if you do choose to root for a particular team, you do so with very little emotional investment—just enough to make the game more exciting. As a result, regardless of which team wins the game, it has nothing to do with you personally, as you have not made rooting for a particular team a part of your identity. The moment the referee blows the whistle that ends the game—regardless of which team wins or loses—you leave the game behind. You walk out of the stadium and continue on with your life, having enjoyed a good game.

In this context, when you watch a game, you are simply enjoying a moment in time without any attachment to the outcome. You experienced the purest form of joy, stemming from your desire to experience the game for the sake of the game, or life without conditions. You maintained your personal freedom throughout the process, as the outcome of the game didn't impact your life one bit.

Keeping with this analogy, let's imagine that you like soccer, but now you are a committed fan of a particular team. Their colors strike an emotional chord inside of you. When the referee blows the whistle, the result of the game affects you on an emotional level. You are elated when your team wins; when your team loses, you feel disappointed.

Your attachment to your team begins to impact your personal life outside the stadium gates as you relate to the world as a fan. For example, when your team loses, you might have a bad day at work, argue with someone about what or who is responsible for the loss, or feel sad despite the many other good things going on around you. No matter what the effect is, you've let your attachment to a particular outcome change your persona. Your attachment to soccer bleeds into a world that has nothing to do with it.

If this attachment is left unchecked, it will become stronger and more entrenched, until the story of victory and defeat of your favorite team is now about *you*. Your team's performance affects your self-worth. When reading the stats, you admonish players for making "us" look bad. If the opposing team wins, you get angry that they beat "you." Not only have you brought the game home, but you have also completely incorporated the game into a part of who you are, shaping your identity by your belief of what it means to be a "real" fan.

Although the soccer team has nothing to do with you in reality, your self-importance correlates with the success or failure of this team because you chose to identify yourself with them in particular. Your life and your attachment to this team are so blurred that you can no longer separate the two, and you believe that anyone who doesn't agree with you about this team is wrong. You might even begin to make loyalty to this team a condition by which you allow others to be in a relationship with you.

If you are having difficulty relating to the sports analogy, let's consider two real-life examples. At the end of one soccer season in Europe, a big-name club was relegated into a lower division after a decisive loss. After witnessing this loss, a fan went home and hung himself. For him, life was no longer worth living if his team wasn't in the Premier League. In another instance, a bus driver was a fan of a losing team, and he was so upset by a particular loss that he drove his bus into a group of people wearing the winning team's jersey. Four people died for wearing the "wrong" colors. This man's attachment to his team was so great that he killed for it. For these two people, the joy of watching soccer for the sake of soccer was lost long ago.

Fortunately, murder and suicide due to a favorite team's loss are very rare occurrences. But when we turn to topics such as religion, politics, money, sex, and power, the negative consequences are far more numerous. When you become attached to an object, idea, or belief, you make it a part of who you think you are. Then, once the fog has you, your vision is obscured. You will no longer see the humanity of an individual who doesn't agree with you, as you can only see the personification of an idea that you stand against.

When your mirror is clear, you can see the divinity in everyone. You can go to any church, synagogue, temple, mosque, or drum circle and find and feel the love and grace of God. For those who are lost in the fog, God just happens to be the focus of devotion that the religion is centered on; in other words, the beliefs and rituals of the religion are more important than experiencing God in the present moment. This is the power of unhealthy attachment.

Understanding the Relationship Between Domestication and Attachment

In the example of the soccer fan, an attachment arose out of something that was genuinely loved: the game of soccer. The fan allowed his love for the game to draw him into the fog, as he made the game part of his identity and confused his association with the team for who he really was.

In the example of the boy and his grandmother, the boy was domesticated to the idea that he must finish all his food, even though that idea wasn't true for him. And as an adult, he adhered to the idea that he should finish his food even if his body is indicating something to the contrary. As a result, he is now also attached to that idea. The difference to understand is this: attachment doesn't always come from domestication, but domestication left unchecked always leads to attachment. Here's what the evolution from domestication to attachment looks like:

1. **Domestication.** You are domesticated to an idea through interaction with others in the Dream of the Planet. (A grandmother domesticates her

grandson to the idea that it's a sin not to finish all the food on his plate.)

2. **Self-domestication.** Once this idea is lodged inside you and accepted, it becomes a belief. You no longer need an outside domesticator to enforce this idea; you will do it yourself. This is self-domestication in action. (The grandson grows up and habitually finishes all the food on his plate even when he isn't hungry.)

3. **Attachment.** You are now attached to this belief, and depending on how strong your attachment is, your acceptance of yourself and others is contingent upon fulfillment of the belief. (The grandson feels guilty if he doesn't finish the food on his plate; he admonishes his friends for not finishing their food, and he domesticates his children to the same idea.)

As you can see, attachments can often arise from domestication. The irony is that when this happens, you become attached to an idea that you didn't even agree with initially but only adopted because of domestication. The end result is that without awareness, you will adhere to ideas that aren't even true for you (as well as push them on others)!

Domestication and attachment work hand in hand to keep you separated from your Authentic Self, lost in the fog and smoke, trapped in the drama of the party. This cycle (domestication, self-domestication, attachment) can continue for generations until you transform into a Master of Self and break the chain. The following exercises will help you begin to identify your own domestications and attachments. Once you have recognized them, you can then decide if you are ready to let them go or not.

◇◇

Noticing Your Domestications

Take a moment to look back over your life. What are some ideas that were instilled in you as a child that you later discarded as no longer true for you? These could be ideas about education and career, money and material possessions, politics, religion, or any number of other areas. Remember, the point here isn't to judge or become resentful of those who initially domesticated you to those ideas, but rather to see where domestication occurred and how you broke free. By noticing where you have already spotted and released domestication in your life, you prove to yourself that you have all the power you need inside you to break free again and again.

Identifying Your Attachments

Since attachment begins with material possessions, the first part of this exercise is designed to show you the items in your life that you have incorporated into your sense of self.

Think of an item you own that you absolutely love, something that you wouldn't want to lose. Perhaps it is your car, your home, your money, an electronic gadget, a piece of jewelry, a special memento, or even a religious or sacred object. The point is to pick an object that you feel strongly about, something that is tied to your sense of self. Very few people who look honestly and deeply will find that there is nothing in the world that doesn't fit this description.

On a blank piece of paper, write down the item and then answer the following questions:

- Why do you feel so strongly about this item?

- What sense of security does it give to you?

- How is this item tied to your identity or sense of self?

- How does it boost your ego?

- Are you pleased to show this item to others? Or it is an item that you show no one and secretly feel special for having?

- Does owning it make you feel more attractive than others, wealthier, more secure, more intelligent, or more spiritual?

Be truthful, reacting honestly from your current emotions. There are no right or wrong answers. The point is to explore your deeper associations with material things.

Now, crumple up the piece of paper and discard it. Close your eyes and imagine that this item no longer exists in your life. How do you feel? What would life be like without it? Who would you be without this item?

Now that you have explored the idea of losing this item, ask yourself the following questions:

- Is this attachment affecting your relationships with the people in your life?

- Is your attachment causing you to play it safe and not pursue other things you really want?

- Can you think of any times when you've altered your actions because of this item?

- How does this attachment affect your personal freedom?

- Finally, do you want to keep this level of attachment? Or do you want to decrease it, or even let it go? The choice is always yours.

As you review your answers, witness the level of fear you experienced at the prospect of losing your item. The more acute the fear, the greater the chance that your attachment will lead to suffering if this item is lost. In the Dream of the Planet one thing is certain: this item will ultimately collapse, corrode, and disappear. Nothing in the Dream lasts forever.

Repeat this exercise and pick a person, belief, role, body image, or idea to examine. This could be your position in the home (father, mother, son), or some other capacity you act in that enhances your sense of self. Are you attached to a particular role you play? How would you feel if that role changed suddenly? Are you attached to how you look? What if your appearance changed overnight? Just like physical objects, beliefs, and social roles, even the people in our lives are destined to change or fall away. Who would you be without them?

If you are like most people, you will find that you are in different levels of attachment with many items, beliefs, and roles, and those levels can fluctuate. Simply becoming aware of these attachments is a big step in releasing their power over you. The moment you become aware of an attachment is the moment it begins to lose its hold over you. Identifying attachments and imagining their collapse gives you the opportunity to see the Authentic Self free from any attachment, as ultimately the truth of who you are is much greater than any item, role, or belief.

◇◇◇

Without awareness, our domestication and attachments blur our perception. Recognizing both allows us to clear the fog and see the truth of the present moment. In the next chapter, we will explore the force that gives domestication and attachments their power, as well as the force that a Master of Self uses to obliterate them.

Chapter Three

Unconditional Love for Yourself

IN THE DREAM OF the Planet there are two powerful forces that shape all our agreements, attachments,
and domestication. In the Toltec tradition, we call these
forces the two types of love: unconditional love and conditional love.

When unconditional love flows from our hearts, we
move through life and engage other living beings with compassion. Unconditional love is recognizing the divinity in
every human being we meet, regardless of his or her role in
life or agreement with our particular way of thinking. A
Master of Self sees all beings through the eyes of unconditional love, without any projected image or distortion.

Conditional love, on the other hand, is the linchpin of domestication and attachment. It only allows you to see what you want to see and to domesticate anyone who doesn't fit your projected image. It's the primary tool used to subjugate those around us and ourselves. Every form of domestication can be boiled down to "If you do this, then I will give you my love" and "If you do not do this, then I will withhold my love." Every form of attachment starts with "If this happens, then I will be happy and feel love" and "If this does not happen, then I will suffer." The key word in all of these statements is *if*, which, as you will see, has no place in unconditional love.

As we construct the Dream of the Planet, we have a choice to love each other unconditionally or conditionally. When we love each other unconditionally, our mirror is clean; we see others and ourselves as we really are: beautiful expressions of the Divine. But when the fog of attachment and domestication clouds our perception and we put conditions on our love, we are no longer able to see the divinity in others and ourselves. We are now competing for a commodity that we have mistaken as love.

At its core, domestication is a system of control, and conditional love is its primary tool. Consequently, the moment you start trying to control others is the same moment you place conditions on your love and acceptance of them. Because you can only give what you have, the conditions you try to impose on others are the same conditions that you impose upon yourself.

When you self-domesticate, you are attempting to control your own actions based on shame, guilt, or perceived reward rather than unconditional self-love. As we saw in the example with the man who continues to eat even after he is full, this is neither a healthy nor happy way to live.

Unconditional love is the antidote to domestication and attachment, and tapping into its power is a key step in becoming a Master of Self. In this chapter we will look at the practice of having unconditional love for ourselves first and foremost, as you cannot give to others what you don't have for yourself.

The Parasite and the Ally

In the Toltec tradition, we refer to the voice in your mind as the narrator, the one that speaks to you throughout your day. When you are self-domesticating, we say that the narrator is acting as a parasite, draining your energy through internal negative self-talk. The voice of the parasite uses your beliefs, formed through domestication and attachment, to hold power over you by placing conditions on your own self-love and self-acceptance. The parasite keeps you trapped in the fog, unable to see the truth of who you really are and the potential that you hold in your heart.

When the voice shares commentary that inspires you to live, create, and love unconditionally, this is constructive self-talk; and in the Toltec tradition we say that the narrator is now acting as an ally, helping you navigate the Dream of the Planet in a peaceful and productive way. When the narrator is your ally, it points out the truth in every situation, reminding you that you are in control of your own life and that you have the ability to make a positive difference in the world. Although the ally is still a reflection of the truth, it is what you see in the mirror when the fog has cleared.

If you are like most people, the narrator in your mind is constantly alternating between parasite and ally, sometimes going back and forth many times during the course of a single day. When the narrator becomes the parasite, doubt sets in, and you question the choices you make. Inspiration and creativity are gone, replaced by self-doubt and conditional self-love. When the ally takes over, you feel confident in your abilities, and the chatter that fills your mind is joyful.

It's important to understand that neither the parasite nor the ally speaks as the Authentic Self. The Authentic Self is the Divine, the energy or spirit that gives life to your body and mind. When you identify with the voice in your head, you confuse the narrator for who you really are and become its slave in the process. When the narrator speaks as your ally, you feel happy, and when the voice of the parasite takes over, you become sad or depressed. But as a Master of Self, you know that neither voice is ultimately you, as neither represents the whole of your Authentic Self.

No words can adequately describe this power that you are, and consequently any voice in your head is not actually you, despite its insistence to the contrary. I'll say it again: you are not your thoughts. Remembering this is important, because when that voice turns ugly and transforms from an ally into a parasite you can recognize it as something learned from some tucked-away experience of domestication and have the confidence to detach from its words. This is the Mastery of Self in action.

Living with the ally is obviously much more pleasant than living with the parasite, and the antidote to spotting and releasing the parasite is having unconditional love for yourself at all times. This, of course, is much easier said than done. The roots of domestication and attachment run deep, and the parasite uses them to stay in control of your mind. Some of you have listened to the parasite for so long you no longer recognize it as a voice of narration that you can disagree with. You have accepted its conclusions as facts, and thereby limit your potential. To undo this, you start by learning how to spot any negative words that enter your field of awareness. As my father taught in the first of the Four Agreements, there is great power in the word, and a Master of Self does not use the power of the word against him- or herself.

Spotting the Parasite

While the parasite operates internally, it strengthens itself by paying attention and latching onto the negative external talk in the Dream of the Planet. Negative external talk is anything you hear in conversation that attempts to impose conditional love. When someone is using the power of his or her words to try to subjugate you, or fill your mind with doubt, this can in turn feed your parasite. Even an offhand remark, in the right (or in this case wrong) tone, can have a powerful effect. "Nice shirt," someone might say sarcastically. The moment before that, you may have been perfectly happy with your shirt; but all of a sudden you begin to internalize the other person's projection, and self-doubt creeps in. Your internal voice becomes negative, and you lose confidence in your choice. You look down and think, "They're right—I don't really like this shirt either." You are now judging yourself based on someone else's opinion. The easiest way for someone to control your will is for you to give them permission to do so, because you doubt your own capacity to make a choice. This is why domestication is so effective.

To be clear, this doesn't mean you don't welcome other people's perspectives and listen to constructive criticism. The difference is in intent. When you are aware of the power of the word, you are careful to separate fact from opinion, and as a Master of Self you decide if the opinion of another is also true for you. When domestication occurs, you listen to others' opinions and mislabel them as facts, accepting them as truth without fully examining them.

The parasite is also strengthened through negative internal talk. This occurs in your Personal Dream when you speak against yourself in your own mind and is commonly referred to as "beating yourself up." In the Toltec tradition, it's understood as the act of using the words of the parasite as conditions for your own self-love and self-acceptance. This internal negativity stems from within. For example, you might look at yourself in the mirror and decide that you're having a bad hair day, or that your pants are looking too tight, or you might find some other physical characteristic to take issue with. Your inner voice may tell you that you don't look good, and you're not going to impress anyone out there.

Without awareness of how you are speaking to yourself you may spiral out of control, and that simple bad hair day can turn into a tirade of negative self-judgments, with you calling yourself ugly, fat, unworthy, etc. In that moment, the parasite has taken over your attention and pulled you deep into the fog, using the power of your word against yourself. If unrecognized, negative talk, both external and internal, can inhibit the power of your intent and lead you deeper into the fog. If you accept the negative talk as fact, without separating truth from opinion, this can become a part of your personal story, leaving the parasite in charge the majority of the time and thereby limiting who you think you are and what you believe you are capable of.

A Master of Self is adept at spotting and releasing the voice of the parasite, and can actually change that voice to one of an ally. Doing so begins with making a commitment to unconditional self-love. This means you become willing to love *every aspect of yourself* without judgment or conditions—especially the parts of yourself that you often wish were different. Unconditional self-love lies within each and every one of us, regardless of our past circumstances and domestication.

We will look at some specific ways to bring unconditional love to yourself in a moment; but before we do, let's be clear on what does not work. First, the parasite cannot defeat itself. In other words, negative self-talk cannot be overcome with more negative self-talk. For example, at my workshops and lectures, people in the past have approached me with a look of consternation and said something like, "I'm so disappointed in myself. I can't believe I have been on the Toltec path for years and I am still taking things personally."

Implicit in the comment is the idea that the speaker is failing in their practice, and you can hear the sneaky voice of the parasite in the background. Were this statement coming through the eyes of unconditional self-love, this person would approach me with a smile instead and say, "You know, I have been on the Toltec path for years, and I notice that I still take things personally sometimes. I am doing my best, but do you have any thoughts on overcoming this hurdle?" The change in the latter is apparent, as the ally is talking instead of the parasite.

The ally speaks from a place of unconditional love, while the parasite speaks from a place of conditional love. Because negative self-talk is based on conditional love, any attempt to transform the parasite with more negative self-talk is a subtle way for the parasite to actually strengthen itself. The key to transforming the parasite into an ally is to bring unconditional love to all of yourself—including the parasite. When you feed the parasite with unconditional love, you transform it into your ally, using the power of your word to change your mind and your life.

The Dream of the Planet is a world of polarities, where something is known only in relation to its opposite. Light is defined in relation to dark, up in relation to down, night to day, etc. Without one, we wouldn't know the other. In instances of opinion, like hot and cold, tall and short, good and bad, assessments are based on our perception, as what is deemed good by one person may be interpreted as bad by someone else. I am aware that when I say something I am both right and wrong at the same time, because the perception of the individual who listens to me will determine the validity of what I say according to their point of view, and they are free to do so. I celebrate that. Thus, I am only responsible for the clarity and integrity of what I say—not what others hear and feel—because I don't control others' perception. This is the incredible power inherent in our minds, and the vehicle we use to express that power is our word.

A Master of Self recognizes the power of the word and knows that every single judgment the parasite utters can be transformed and used by the ally. Making the switch to do so is unconditional self-love in action. While many people choose to listen to and focus on the voice of the parasite, it's critical that you train your mind to see through the eyes of the ally. There is no better place to do this than in your own personal story.

My friend and teaching partner, HeatherAsh Amara, has a beautiful example in her book *Warrior Goddess Training* of how she consciously changed her narrator from the parasite to the ally. Here is the parasite perspective she began with:

I was traumatized as a child by how often my family moved. I went to eight different schools and lived in four countries—Singapore, Hong Kong, the United States, and Thailand—by the time I was sixteen. We would move every two years or so. I started off at each school feeling painfully shy, disconnected, and alone. By the second year I would have made friends and found my groove, and then we would move again and the cycle would start over. Because of the many times I moved away from friends, I have a hard time connecting with people intimately and I'm afraid of being abandoned.

Every time I told my story, I felt depressed. Wouldn't you?

After HeatherAsh began her apprenticeship with my father, she began to see and tell her story through the eyes of the ally. Notice the shift in perspective, based on the same facts:

> I was blessed as a child with an adventurous family. We moved every two years and traveled around the world every summer. I spent most of my childhood going to great international schools in Southeast Asia, and by the time I was sixteen my family had visited or lived in twenty different countries, including Thailand, Singapore, India, Egypt, Italy, and Spain. Because of the many times we moved and traveled, I learned to be incredibly flexible and to deeply love the diversity and creativity of humans. My childhood experiences helped me relate to many different perspectives, to make friends easily, and to celebrate change.
>
> Each time I told this new story, I felt a sense of adventure and lots of gratitude.

As you can see, the facts stay the same, but the story is dramatically different. Do you see the power of perception?

The following exercises will help you practice transforming your parasite into your ally.

◇◇

Releasing Judgment

Look at yourself in the mirror and notice all the self-judgments that arise in the next few moments. Does a voice inside you say that your nose is too big? Too small? Do you not like your body size? Or your complexion? Take a moment to listen to those judgments. Your emotions will let you know which ones affect you the most, as the stronger the negative feeling the more attached you are to that judgment.

Write the judgment that incites the strongest emotional response on a piece of paper. It's very important that you write this down (you'll understand why in a moment). Next, take a moment to remember the many instances when you have used this judgment against yourself. Perhaps this thought has been repeating in your mind for years and years.

Now you can investigate the source of this judgment, and identify how it has affected your actions in the Dream of the Planet. Underneath the judgment, write down your answers to the following questions:

- Is this a judgment you learned from someone else? Can you remember when you learned it, and from whom?

- Have you repeated this judgment about yourself to someone else?

- How has this judgment shaped your actions? Have you denied yourself opportunities or failed to take risks because of it?

Read your responses and then ask yourself this very important question:

- Do you still want to let this judgment control your life?

If after reading all of your responses you answer yes to this last question, then this is an attachment that has become a part of your identity. It shapes who you are, and you are not ready to let it go. This is fine, if it is truly what you want. Perhaps you will come back to this at a later point to find that you no longer need this belief.

If you answered no to this last question, then you see the written judgment as something that is not a part of you; it is a piece of paper with words on it, nothing more. Realize that this judgment is only in front of you now because you have implicitly agreed with it all along. Now, the time has come to let this go, and the first step is to forgive yourself for using it against you all those times.

When you are ready to release this judgment, say the following statement out loud:

"I, _____, have used my negative self-talk to subjugate myself with conditional love. I forgive myself for doing so, and I will now let this false belief go."

Crumple up the paper and throw it in the trash. This is a sacred act of letting this false belief go because you no longer believe it. Remember, beliefs don't exist "out there" in the world; they exist only in your mind and only as long as you continue to believe.

Every time find yourself falling back into self-judgment on this issue, repeat this statement of forgiveness again. Doing so is the act of bringing unconditional love to yourself. You have already paid the price for this self-judgment; you don't need to do so anymore. As my father says, true justice is paying for something once; injustice is paying for it over and over again. Through self-forgiveness you can stand up and start fresh. Self-forgiveness is always the key, and unconditional self-love gives you that opportunity. Repeat this exercise when you are ready for each and every judgment you listed initially.

Changing the Attributes

What stories are you carrying around about past events? Do you recount these stories through the eyes of your parasite or your ally? Think about the story of your life for a moment. What are the main elements? How do you tell that story to yourself and others? Notice the places in your story that you often tell through the eyes of the parasite, and write that portion of your story down.

Next, rewrite that same portion of your story, but this time through the eyes of your ally. (See the excerpt from my friend Heather-Ash Amara earlier in the chapter as an example.) If you are like most people, you'll find it's often easier to write through the eyes of the parasite than the ally, and this demonstrates the power that domestication, attachment, and conditional love have over you. Writing from the ally's perspective can be more difficult, but reframing your life events in this way allows you to see the gifts in every past experience.

◇◇

In the end, our narrators are simply storytellers. They tell stories about the events in our lives and interpret them in either a positive or negative way, depending upon which one is in charge. A Master of Self sees the events of life through the eyes of the ally instead of the parasite, as doing so is a way of expressing unconditional self-love; this is the power you have to direct and redirect your attention to and from different focal points. Once you have unconditional love for yourself, you can then offer it to others. This is the subject of the next chapter.

Chapter Four

Unconditional Love for Others

As a Master of Self, when I look into the eyes of another individual I see another Authentic Self, a beautiful expression of the Divine. No matter where this person is in the process of awakening, I respect that his or her intent is just as powerful as mine, and doing so is an act of unconditional love. If I were to try to control this person, I would be lost in the fog and place conditions on my love and acceptance of him or her.

If you see the world through the eyes of conditional love, you are by definition attempting to control others, imposing your will so that they conform to the definition of who and what you think they should be. If they don't agree to your demands, they will receive the punishment of your judgment. This is conditional love in a nutshell. But remember, every time you judge someone you are punishing that person for not following agreements they never made.

As you look back over your life, you can see that many of the relationship battles you thought were for your own personal freedom were really battles of who was going to domesticate whom. And every time you experienced a moment of anger, outrage, indignation, or any other negative emotion as the result of someone else's behavior, you created a dream of villains and victims, and you were once again caught in the drama of the party.

Perceiving yourself as a victim and another as a villain doesn't allow you to see the person who is actually standing before you: you don't see their story, their past, their heartbreaks, and how all of that has impacted their life and contributed to forming the person you're talking to. All you can see through the fog of domestication is that the person you have cast as the villain in your story isn't living up to the values you think they should.

But when you see another with the eyes of unconditional love, you are then able to clearly see who is actually in front of you, a living being who is trying to survive and thrive in a world filled with domestication and conditional love. Unconditional love allows you to disagree with the choices or beliefs of others while still respecting their right to have them.

Practicing unconditional love is the art of the Master of Self. Once you have recognized, released, and forgiven the self-judgments that have arisen from your own domestication, you can then recognize and forgive others when they act from their domestication. The person in front of you has been domesticated, and now they want to pass that on to you because it's all they know. However, they can only subjugate you with your permission.

For many people, family can present a unique challenge to seeing through the eyes of unconditional love, because it is here that the roots of domestication are deepest. Often it's the wounds that you have with your family that hurt the most, but the reason they hurt so much is because you love them. This deep love is also what will help you to forgive and heal.

Next to your family, your most influential domesticators growing up were probably your friends and classmates. These are the people you wanted to impress, or to be like, so you often tried to adjust your behavior according to what they found acceptable. And, of course, you likely asked the same of them. This doesn't mean that there wasn't also genuine love present for these friends, but because you all came from homes rooted in domestication it was all you knew, and you brought these practices into your relationships.

There comes a point in life when we wake up from the Dream and we begin to choose friends who accept us, encourage us to grow, and support us—and we are willing to do the same from them. But if we don't continue to recognize where and how domestication has affected us, and work to spot and release it when it arises, the same patterns will develop with our new friendships: we will ultimately place conditions on them to fit into our new model, however "enlightened" we think it to be. For instance, I will sometimes hear comments in Toltec circles like, "that person isn't a good Toltec," or "she isn't impeccable with her word." In these cases, you can hear how the tools of enlightenment have been turned into sources of judgment, control, and domestication.

In all our relationships, but especially our relationships with our friends and family, where the roots of domestication run the deepest, our job is to be aware of our potential to get hooked back into the drama of the party, to be blinded by the fog, and the key to avoiding this is to continually remind ourselves to act from a place of unconditional love. This is easier said than done, especially when the roots of domestication run deep, but there is a way.

Creating Peace in the Dream of the Planet

When you find yourself in a disagreement with someone and you can feel you're getting upset, you have a decision as to what you do or say next. Before you speak or take another action, ask yourself this question: is what I am about to say or do coming from a place of conditional love or unconditional love? In other words, is your love and acceptance of the person in front of you somehow contingent upon them agreeing with you or doing what you wish? If so, that is your cue that your domestication and attachments are in control of you, and now you are trying to domesticate someone else to your point of view. If your response is from unconditional love, by definition your response shows the other person respect, even if you ultimately disagree with their views or actions. Mutual respect is the key that allows true peace to occur in the Dream of the Planet. This respect also allows everyone to experience the benefits and consequences of their own choices and actions.

When conditional love dominates the Dream of the Planet, any semblance of peace and harmony occurs through force, when one person or persons subjugate the will of others. Governments are famous for this type of behavior, and history is littered with examples of one group controlling another through the belief that "might makes right." But this also occurs in personal relationships, when one person uses a position of power to control the behavior of another. This, of course, is not real peace and harmony, and it never lasts. People will always rebel against subjugation and fight to reclaim their free will. Because our very nature itself is freedom we will always strive for it—even when our vision is clouded by the fog.

The problem is that if a group of people fights for freedom without clearing their own fog first, that is, their domestication and attachments, these same people who gained freedom from an oppressor will eventually replace the previous set of conditions with their own, and in turn try to subjugate the people around them in order to establish their vision of peace and harmony. This cycle of imposition and subjugation has been occurring in the Dream of the Planet for thousands of years. This is how wars begin, end, and start again, and this is true no matter if it's a brawl on the street or an international conflict, as both stem from one party's desire to subjugate the other, based on the subjugator's belief that their way is the "right" way. This is the cycle that conditional love always produces.

Peace and harmony from the point of view of unconditional love are the engagement of equals, using knowledge and awareness to co-create a dream whose diversity reflects the free will of each individual living in this moment. Much like the party where you are the only sober person, you cannot expect everyone to want to be sober, or to want to wake up. Nor can you make anyone do so. Attempting to wake someone up against their will is attempting to subjugate them to your ideas.

So how do we engage from a place of unconditional love? How do we sincerely try to help others awaken without subjugating them? Taking a moment to reflect and discern what your true motivations are is not always easy, especially when you are in the heat of the moment and the drama of the party is trying to hook you back into believing the Dream is real. Furthermore, coming from a place of unconditional rather than conditional love may still involve doing or saying something that the other person doesn't like; but speaking your truth from a place of love and respect is the Mastery of Self in action.

It's at these times that I remember something my father taught me: "I am responsible for what I say, but I am not responsible for what you hear." I am responsible to the tips of my fingers and no further, and how someone reacts to what I say or do is out of my control. Of course, this truth is not meant to be a license to say or do something that is unkind or intentionally hurtful (to be considerate of others is also a choice we have), but we understand that when we break the chains of our domestication, this news can be hard for our domesticators and those trying to domesticate us to handle, especially at first.

What really matters is our intention. When we come from a place of unconditional love, we can have the confidence that whatever action we take is the right one, and the outcome of any situation is beyond our control. We do the best we can, and we release our attachment to the outcome. This can be difficult to do at first, and even a little scary. But committing to act from a place of unconditional love eases this anxiety, as we know that our actions, and our actions after that, are coming from a place that is true to our being.

Overcoming Resentment and Forgiving Others

When you look back and review the beliefs, ideas, and conditions that you have tried to live up to, you often realize that their origin resides in the domestication you experienced in the past. This can be a very troubling realization for some of you, depending on the level of subjugation you experienced growing up. If those with power inflicted their will on you via force or manipulation, and especially if the subjugation was harsh or even extreme, it can be very difficult—and almost impossible in some cases—to see them through the eyes of unconditional love. Even for those of you who didn't have a particularly traumatic experience with domestication, there are very few people who don't have some anger or bitterness over incidents that occurred during their formative years.

Resentments that stem from past domestication are some of the biggest stumbling blocks to seeing others through the eyes of unconditional love. The word *resentment* is French in origin, and it literally means "to feel again." One of the primary benefits of doing this work is that you no longer allow any conditioning or experience from the past to control you in the present. By definition, if you are holding on to resentment, then you are enslaved to the past. Something that has occurred, is already done, is actively causing you suffering now as you feel it again and again. This is what resentment is: self-inflicted suffering with the emotional poison we wish for another.

Anger, resentment, and grudges are all tools that the parasite uses to strengthen itself and take control of your mind, and here again its methods are very sneaky. Because while the parasite may accurately point out how you were mistreated at the hands of another, the solution it offers is to stir up the negative emotions of anger, sadness, bitterness, etc., and encourage you to at best withhold your love from those who hurt you, and at worst to strike back at them with revenge. The parasite always reaches for the tools of conditional love, and no ultimate good ever comes from employing them. Instead you are lost in the fog again, and your Dream is tied to a story of victims and villains.

Unconditional love and forgiveness of your domesticators is the way out. This can be some of the most difficult work you will do, so be gentle with yourself as you embark on this road, especially if you suffered greatly at the hands of others.

In addition to forgiving those who harmed you, you also need to forgive yourself. That's because many people, when they look deeply at past experiences of domestication, find that they are angry with themselves for either staying in a situation or not doing more to break free. If this applies to you, remember to forgive yourself for that too. You were doing the best you could at the time; there is no need to beat yourself up.

Respecting yourself also means being honest with yourself. If you are not ready to forgive, that is your truth. Don't subjugate yourself with "I have to." If you are not ready, you are not ready; and the acceptance of yourself with this truth is practicing unconditional love. After all, it is about breaking the cycle of domestication. Take your time, if it's your preference, to become ready to heal. Forgiving is the final step of healing a wound.

Performing a forgiveness ritual can help you clean out old emotions that are keeping you trapped in the suffering of the past (we will do just that in the exercises that follow), and many of the world's beautiful spiritual traditions provide wonderful prayers and other practices for doing so. In the Toltec tradition we also advocate another step to see beyond the stories of villains and victims and into the healing power of forgiveness. The key to doing this is at the heart of my father's third agreement: don't take things personally.

When you practice this agreement in all its implications, you realize that nothing anyone does is because of you. It's never personal, even if someone intends it to be so, as you are simply standing in the target zone. Seeing the truth of this allows you to better let go of the past and embrace the truth of the moment: your domesticators were only doing the best they could given their level of consciousness at the time.

When you reflect on this agreement deeply, forgiveness comes much easier because you realize that the actions of others were about them and their suffering, their attachments, and their domestications, and you see that they were lost in the fog, drunk at the party, and as a result they didn't have the faculties to act in any other way. Respect them, and allow them to experience the consequence of their actions. For every action, there is an equal and opposite reaction. It is the way that life teaches us. Seen in this light, we can better grasp the meaning of Jesus' statement, "Father, forgive them, for they know not what they do" (Luke 23:34).

If you have clouded your Personal Dream with resentment, the first step to changing this is to become aware of it. Once you see what is really happening, the next step to moving past it is forgiveness. Doing so allows you to tap into the power of unconditional love for others. The next exercises will help you go deeper into this process.

◇◇◇

Forgiveness Ritual

On a sheet of paper, make a list of everyone you feel has mistreated you in the past that you have not yet forgiven. This list could include members of your family, friends, coworkers, acquaintances, and beyond. Review the list of names and think briefly about the incidents involved.

Next, read the following statement out loud:

"I, _____, am ready to forgive all those who inflicted pain and suffering on

me in the past. I choose to forgive them so that their actions of the past can no longer affect my present. My wish is to see them through the eyes of unconditional love. I also forgive myself for anything and everything related to these events. I was doing my best at the time. I pray that these people, and myself, can experience only love and peace going forward."

Just as you did in the preceding chapter's exercise when you forgave yourself, I want you to take the piece of paper, crumple it up, and throw it away. As you do so, visualize all the negative feelings you have about these people and the events going in the trash as well.

This simple ritual is the beginning of replacing resentment with unconditional love for those who have caused you suffering. That being said, when the pain inflicted by others is extreme, an act of forgiveness is rarely a onetime event. As a result, you will likely need to repeat the aforementioned statement every time the events of your past replay in your mind and you feel them again, as the parasite is attempting to lead you down the road of negativity and conditional love.

If there is someone on the list who you are having special trouble forgiving, say the prayer below every night before you go to bed, inserting the name of the person or persons you'd like to forgive:

"I pray that _____ receives everything they want in life, including the experience of unconditional love, peace, and happiness."

Some of you likely bristled as you read this, as the prospect of praying that these people receive everything they want is perhaps the opposite of what you think you want for them. I understand this sentiment, but I would encourage you to give this prayer a chance, and repeat it every night for two weeks even if the words don't feel sincere. Many people who have done this exercise consistently for two weeks have been amazed by the changes that occur inside them.

Remember, forgiving others is something you're doing for yourself, not for them. Forgiveness does not mean that you forget the events of the past, nor that you condone any actions; rather, it frees you from being controlled by them by remembering that you are only responsible to the tips of your own fingers. The final exercise in this section will help you continue on the path of forgiveness.

Forgiveness Dialogue

PART 1

This exercise consists of two written parts, each about a paragraph in length. To begin, I want you to look back over your life and identify an event or situation where you experienced significant suffering at the hands of another. Think of a time when someone either tried to or did domesticate you by forcing their will onto you in a harsh or extreme way. This should be a major event that created a shift in your Personal Dream, that changed the way you viewed others, likely exposing their flaws, and ended up becoming a defining moment in your personal story. Many people have experienced something like this, most likely during their formative years, but it could also be something that occurred as an adult.

Write down the details of the event as if you were going to tell someone who had no previous knowledge of it. Take your time and replay the details in your mind, going back to that moment so you can remember what happened and how you felt. And here is the important part: write from your perspective at the time, not from where you are now. Be raw and in the moment, let your feelings flow, and do not edit yourself with knowledge of what is right and wrong or try to be forgiving. Remember, this exercise is for you, and unless you choose to share this with someone else, you will be the only person who ever sees it.

Here is an example from a dear friend of mine:

One night when I was nine years old, I was at home watching TV when I heard my parents start to argue in the other room. I had heard them fight before, but tonight seemed different. My mother came in and told me to go to my room and close the door, which was not unusual. I did as I was told, and sat quietly and fearfully in my room, listening through the thin walls as their shouts grew louder and louder. Then I heard something I will never forget: a bloodcurdling scream from my mother followed by an eerie silence. I froze in panic, wanting to leave my room but afraid of what I would find if I did.

I opened the door and went down the hall to the family room. My father was sitting alone on the couch, and when he saw me, he said, "Your mother ran out of the house. Go see if you can find her." I remember being scared of him and angry with him at the same time, but my main concern was my mother. I went outside to look for her. It was dark and I was afraid. I looked into the darkness and called out to her, but she didn't respond. Then I noticed the neighbor's porch light was on.

As I walked over toward the porch, I could hear voices and my mother sobbing. I asked her what happened, but in my heart I already knew. "Your father hit me," she said. "He beats me." I was overcome with a combination of rage and sadness, and I swore to protect my mother if he ever tried to do that again. "If he ever does that again, I'll kill him," I said. That evening was life-changing for me, as for the first time in my life the dark side of my father was in full view. He took his own life six months later.

In my friend's case, his father was attempting to domesticate his mother (and in conjunction my friend) through the use of force. Your example might not be as extreme, or it could be more so. To get the most out of this exercise, I encourage you to not read any farther until you have written down the example in your own life. Once you have, come back and continue with the exercise.

PART 2

This next part involves your imagination. I want you to imagine that you are meeting the person who hurt you in their spiritual form only. In this meeting you can talk directly to the other person's Authentic Self, the part of them that is awake, not lost in the fog or drunk at the party. In this form, they are imbued with unconditional love, and you can say whatever you want without fear. Tell them how you really feel about them and the situation, and then imagine what this person would say to you from the perspective of their Authentic Self. Write that dialogue out between the two of you.

Here is my friend's example:

Dad, I am so angry and saddened by what happened. I can't believe you would hit your wife like that. You scared me so bad. We are best friends, and I looked up to you so much. I can't understand how you would do that. What is the matter with you? When you drink, you are such a different person. I feel guilty that I wasn't there to try to stop you. When you died a few months later, I was sad, but also a little relieved, because I knew I wouldn't have to worry about your violence anymore. I couldn't help but feel guilty for feeling relieved by your death too.

Son, I am so sorry for hurting your mother and you. I completely lost control of myself. I didn't know what I was doing. When I drink, I am not myself. Please know that I want only the best for you and your mother. I love you both dearly, and if I could take back that moment I would. I am so very sorry, and I ask for your forgiveness. You have absolutely nothing to feel guilty about. I am responsible for that entire situation, so I want you to let all of that go right now. Please know that from

*where I am now, I have only love for you
and your mother, and I am doing my best
to help you from afar.*

This exercise allows you to get in touch with your feelings at the time, express them, and then listen to the response from the other person, spoken from the perspective of his or her Authentic Self. The result for most people is that they are better able to see and understand that the actions of the other person weren't personal, and that at the heart of every individual is unconditional love.

◇◇

Remember to be gentle with yourself as you explore and release these past events that have caused you pain. This can be difficult, but the truth is that the tougher it is, the more you stand to gain. The freedom you will experience will profoundly affect your life going forward, and it's very difficult to progress on your path without going through this important step of forgiveness. Take it slow and return to these exercises when you need to, going a little deeper each time.

Chapter Five

Spotting the Triggers
and Maneuvering the Traps

UP UNTIL THIS POINT in this book, the information presented has been largely foundational. That's because in the process of becoming a Master of Self, one begins by understanding that we are dreaming, both on a personal and a collective level. Once the Dream is recognized, we turn our attention to those things that can make the Dream a nightmare, specifically domestication and attachment, which you'll remember are fueled by conditional love. We also learned that the antidote to the nightmare is unconditional love, and the key to accessing that type of love lies in forgiveness for others and ourselves.

But information alone doesn't make you a master. Applying the tools does, and this is where we will now turn our focus. As you live life, engaging and interacting with others rather than sitting alone in a cloistered monastery, you are sure to encounter many situations that have the potential to hook your attention and knock you off-balance. The Dream of the Planet is full of these types of traps, and falling into them pulls you out of your awareness and back into the fog and drama of the party.

One of the pillars of the Mastery of Self is learning to spot the triggers and maneuver the traps that are waiting to hook you, and nothing can help you more in this process than becoming aware of your emotions.

Understanding Your Emotions

Our emotions are wonderful tools. Being in touch with them allows us to experience life to the fullest. When we are aware, our emotions can teach us a variety of things. They can show us what we like and don't like, what's really important to us as opposed to what isn't, and they can provide a wonderful guide to discovering the work we are meant to do in the Dream of the Planet.

For instance, when you are faced with an important decision and you are unsure of which course of action to take, one thing that can help you is to focus on how you feel about the options presented instead of being consumed with the stories your narrators are spouting. As you get to know yourself better, this type of discernment becomes a very effective tool for recognizing what you really want. In popular vernacular, this would be referred to as "listening to your heart instead of your head," but it's really the Mastery of Self in action.

Your emotions can also show you where you are still holding on to attachments and reveal any remaining fears and self-doubts from past domestications that you haven't yet released. Sometimes you won't even realize you have an attachment until an event triggers an emotional reaction in you. Anytime you feel a burst of anger, frustration, guilt, shame, or any number of other negative emotions, that's your cue to look within and see what is happening. Ask yourself questions like, Where is this feeling coming from? When have I experienced this before? What is the source of this feeling? Once you are aware of what's happening inside, you are able to calm yourself and stop the downward spiral before you lose control.

While anger is a common emotional reaction, it is by no means the only one. Shutting down, being defensive or passive-aggressiveness, feeling guilty or remorseful, or any unhelpful reactions in between are additional ways in which you can react emotionally and lose awareness of your Authentic Self.

Whether your tendency is to be consumed with anger and rage or to sulk silently in the corner, the underlying cause of all of these emotional reactions is always fear, the tool of conditional love. When fear overtakes you and sparks an emotional reaction, your attachments and domestications are now running the show, and unconditional love is cast to the wayside. Becoming a Master of Self is about noticing when you begin to have an emotional reaction and asking yourself immediately, "What am I afraid of?" The quicker you can identify and release the fear, the faster you become re-grounded in the Authentic Self.

Any emotional reaction you experience is yours, not anyone else's, and consequently it is here to teach you something about yourself. The Master of Self sees this as an opportunity to learn and grow, and in doing so you can deal with these emotions before they lead to an outburst that causes harm to your Personal Dream or the Dream of the Planet.

Conflict in the Dream of the Planet

Because there are over seven billion Personal Dreams happening concurrently in the Dream of the Planet, disagreements are inevitable. But these disagreements can also serve a very healthy purpose, as they challenge each of us to continually evolve our respective Personal Dreams. When one person, not to mention both parties, has an emotional reaction as a result of a disagreement, the possibility to see things from the point of view of the other closes, and conflict begins. An emotional reaction leaves you stuck, unable to move forward until you look more deeply at whatever the emotion is trying to tell you.

Every Master of Self—even those who have implemented these tools diligently for years—will come across certain people and situations that pose special challenges. These are the people who can really push your buttons, and dealing with them is likely to discharge an emotional reaction. While you may be able to avoid dramatic or anxiety-provoking people and situations in many instances, there will always be those moments when you can't walk away, when you just have to deal with the person or situation at hand right then.

The question then becomes, Can you engage without being drawn back into the drama of the party? Can you stay grounded in your Authentic Self and show the other person respect? As a Master of Self who wants to maintain control of his or her will and have unconditional love for all in the Dream of the Planet, you can stay balanced much more easily if you find out why this person has the unique ability to provoke a reaction in you. Think about it. Of all the people in the entire world, this person can push your buttons maybe better than anybody else. This is a very special gift they are offering you, and freedom awaits as soon as you can find out why that is. In my experience, the root can often be traced to one of three things (and sometimes more than one simultaneously). Let's look at those now.

1. **Prior domestication.** It's possible that the person or situation provokes a deep memory of someone attempting to domesticate you and you resisting. Even if you can't fully remember the event, your subconscious or deep memory is making the connection. As a result, your perception of the current situation is skewed by the domestication of the past. You are seeing this person as a potential threat, and your conscious or unconscious mind has labeled them as such, even if you don't realize it.

If you can connect the dots and see that the reason this person bothers you is based on a past experience rather than the current situation, you have begun to eliminate their power to upset you, putting your will back into your control.

With the knowledge of the memory or similar situation that the person is activating in you, you can work toward forgiving and releasing the trauma caused by the past domesticator and see the current situation in a new light, no longer obscured by the shadow of your past. Often just the association with the past begins to free you from the torment of the present situation, thus removing its power over you and absolving it as a potential trigger.

2. **Mirroring.** Everyone is our mirror, and our reflection of things we don't like about ourselves is most vivid in those who have the same qualities. In other words, you may see a piece of yourself in this other person even if you don't realize it. This truth may come as a surprise to some of you, and your initial reaction may be to disagree. But I invite you to look deeper. Whatever characteristic you see in another that you don't like is often a characteristic you see in some degree in yourself. For instance, if you catch someone in a lie and that bothers you greatly, can you find a time in your past where you have also been a liar? If you find yourself complaining about the

shortcomings of your friends, notice how many of those complaints could also apply to you. This can be a hard truth to swallow at first, but it is also a useful tool to dissolve any negative internal reaction that occurs when dealing with someone else, because it allows you to see him or her as yourself.

3. **Attachment.** When you encounter someone who has an uncanny ability to provoke a reaction in you, it may be because you have an attachment to a belief that you feel needs to be defended, and you view this other person as a threat to that belief. When you are very attached to your beliefs, conflicts are almost certain to arise.

While some beliefs may need defending, especially when they involve the physical well-being of yourself or someone else, these are typically not the ones we find ourselves in conflict over. There is a big difference between defending a belief that protects your physical being and a belief that simply supports a position your ego holds dear. Knowing the difference between the two, as well as your commitment to respecting another's right to believe differently than you, is a way to release your attachment to a belief grounded in egotism and view the other person's viewpoint with respect.

Putting the Mastery of Self into Action

The next time you are in a situation and you begin to feel angry, defensive, guilty, sad, or anything similar arising, the first step is to spot the emotion. Admit it exists, and accept that these feelings are inside you. Just identifying, admitting, and accepting the feelings often has a calming effect and begins the process of releasing them. The next questions to ask yourself are:

- What is this emotion here to show you?
- What fears are the words or actions of another activating inside you?
- What are you trying to control, and why?

In most cases, the answer will fall into the category of past domestication, mirroring, or attachments.

A Master of Self recognizes that any negative emotions that are arising are really a gift, an opportunity for discovery, as no one else is responsible for your emotional reactions except you. This last sentence bears repeating: *No one else is responsible for your emotional reactions except you.* Others can say and do anything they like, but what happens inside you is only the result of what you are thinking and feeling.

Sometimes you may find yourself in a situation where you have a negative emotion that you can't immediately identify the origin of, and even when you can, you are not able to release it because you can feel the emotion building. In those cases, restrain yourself from doing or saying anything at that moment if that is an option. Then remove yourself from the situation until you have more clarity. Let no one tell you that being a Master of Self does not involve willpower, as in certain situations exercising restraint may require all the willpower you have.

In some instances, taking a break may not be possible, and you find yourself face-to-face with a person or thing that is causing an emotional reaction to rise up inside you, and you decide to deal with the situation immediately as it presents itself. This is when respect and unconditional love come into play. Through the power of your will, remember that the other person is worthy of your respect, which is not to take responsibility for their will by trying to impose your own will upon them—even if you disagree with their position. Remember that this person is seeing the world through their own point of view, domesticated or not. By maintaining respect and unconditional love for the other person, you can remain calm in the moment and speak your truth with love.

Again, the quick-check question to ask yourself before you speak is this: is what I am about to say coming from me or from my domesticated beliefs? If your statement is trying to impose a condition on the other, then I encourage you to look within and find new words. If you are coming from a place of awareness, whatever words come out of your mouth will be the right ones. Remember, coming from a place of unconditional love does not mean we say things that the other person will agree with or enjoy, but in those moments we remember that we cannot control the other person's perception or reaction; we only have control over ourselves.

Sometimes exiting the situation and not returning is the best option to avoid further conflict. When the other person no longer respects you, they will try to subjugate you to their will. To maintain respect for yourself, it is often wise to walk away before your emotions take over and you do or say something you will later regret. Exiting like this is not running from your problems or emotions, but rather a prudent decision rooted in self-care, as engaging further wouldn't be helpful for either party. A martial arts master will tell you that your mind is your most powerful weapon and your first line of defense. It takes discipline to use a fist to defend your physical body and not be tempted to become the tyrant of aggression. Always be aware of what lies on the other side of self-respect.

The alternative to the above is to allow your emotions to control you, and to lash out in anger, overreact with defensiveness, or anywhere in between. At that moment you are drawn back into the drama of the party, lost in the smoke and fog again. The result of this type of behavior is always the same; you create suffering for yourself and others in the Dream of the Planet.

Modern Triggers

The modern world presents some interesting new ways to trigger emotional reactions. I imagine that most of you reading this are familiar with social media sites like Facebook, Twitter, etc., as well as text messaging. Social media and text messaging have connected us in a way that we have never seen before in the Dream of the Planet. While social media can help us stay in touch with those we have a bond with, it has also become fertile ground for emotional reactions to digital conversations, and consequently social media sites sometimes seem more like an emotional minefield than an electronic playground.

The good news is that this technology gives you another valuable tool for self-exploration, as you can notice the assumptions that you make about others. In other words, since you can't see the facial expressions or the body language of someone when they post something on social media or send a text message, your mind's first reaction is to often make an assumption of their meaning through your projection of their intention. In this way, you can fill in the blank by projecting an emotion onto a comment, post, or message that was maybe not intended by the person who wrote it. Social media and text messaging allow you to notice what emotions you project or assume are intended by the other person, and investigate what internal domestications and attachments are at the source of your assumptions.

Remember, being a Master of Self does not mean we are robots without feelings, or that we never take the bait and react emotionally. But when you give away control of your will via an emotional reaction instead of a conscious response, practicing these tools allows you to recover quickly. Acknowledging that you feel anger, jealousy, resentment, sadness, and such allows you to see the truth of how you feel right now. The realization can take just a second or a night's tossing and turning in bed, but the downward spiral ends the moment you surrender to the truth. When you find the true source of the emotion (usually some prior domestication or current attachment), you can use that knowledge as an instrument of transformation.

Every time you fall into a trap and react instead of respond, ask yourself, What am I afraid of? Once you know this, you can look deeper to find out where the fear comes from. Emotional reactions will always pop up and have power over you until you deal with the unresolved fears that hide underneath. The good news is that once you find out what you are afraid of and release that fear, the situation no longer has power over you.

◇◇◇

Resolving Conflicts

In the Dream of the Planet, people will often not act the way you want them to, or the way you think they should. They will not always agree with your ideas or your beliefs. This begs the question, how do you react when others don't behave the way you'd like them to? Do you try to impose your will and subjugate them to your point of view? Or are you able to step back and respect their point of view?

This exercise will help you find out. To begin, think of any recent conflict you've had with another person. This could be something that happened at home, work, school, etc.— any instance where you and someone else had opposing viewpoints. Briefly write down the conflict on a sheet of paper. Then answer the following questions:

- In this conflict, what belief were you trying to subjugate the other person to? (This is not an evaluation of whether a belief is "right" or "wrong"; the purpose is to become aware of what the belief is.)

- Do you know where this belief came from?

- Is this a belief you want to maintain? There are no right or wrong answers here. It's fine if the belief is true for you, and it's fine if it's not; the point is to know so that you don't continue to fight for a belief you no longer believe in, as this is domestication in action.

- How did you treat the other person when they didn't agree with you? Did you respect their point of view, or did you try to coerce them into seeing things your way?

- What do you think the other person's belief is? Can you see another perspective on this same situation? Can you see how the other person's belief is true for them?

- ◆ How do you want to act the next time a conflict like this arises? Is there a way you can engage with the other person, be true to yourself, and not try to change or subjugate the other person?

As a Master of Self, you know avoiding all conflict is impossible, so when conflicts arise, your job is to look within, see what is true for you in the moment, and find a way to honor your own beliefs while simultaneously respecting the choices and beliefs of others. Return to this exercise whenever you experience a conflict with another person.

The Transformative Power of Listening

The following exercise will help you stay grounded and in touch with your emotions. The focus is on listening to the people in your life who have different beliefs and values than you.

Find someone you are close to and ask them a question on a topic you know you disagree on. Then listen. This is not the place for you to share your own opinions. Just listen. Ask the person to expand on their opinion without challenging or belittling it, and as they speak be sure to do the following:

Look at the person's body language as they speak. Notice how their facial expressions and mannerisms change when they are simply trying to share their opinion versus persuade or convert you. How do you feel as they move between sharing knowledge and persuading? Can you feel the difference within yourself? This is where your reactions to the topic stem from—not their words, but from within.

Try to understand where they are coming from. As you listen, keep in mind that they likely have an experience or domestication that colors their worldview. Instead of seeing their view as wrong, try to see where it comes from, and understand their attachments. After all, it does not matter if you are right.

Listen without planning your reply. Try to hear what the person is saying without thinking of a reply. If you put your attention on your reply as they are talking, then you are not really listening. By not formulating a response, you are better able to listen without your projection getting in the way.

Express your opinion only after the person has finished talking, and only if they ask. First let the person know that you value their point of view. Next, identify and summarize any points that you may agree on. Doing so is a sign of respect and lets the other know they were heard, and may set the stage for them to show you respect in return. Last, offer your perspective with respect.

Notice your own attachments. Finally, use this exercise as a way to listen and perceive the world from a different point of view, whether you agree with it or not, and notice if your own attachments are clouding your view. In other words, could this person be right about any of their points?

Feel your emotions. Notice any negative emotions that come up for you while you are listening. For instance, do you experience fear? Anger? Sadness? What is the source of these emotions? If these emotions arise for you, finding their origin is where you will find your gift.

If you practice this exercise with your family and friends, it will help you engage others with respect and maintain awareness of your emotions as you do so. If family is too much, then practice with your outer circle of friends and work your way toward your inner circle. Not only will this help you foster respect for others, but you will become more aware of the beliefs and attachments that guide your Personal Dream. You may also become more open to those who are different than you or who share a different worldview, moving toward acceptance of all others without biases or conditions.

Controlling Your Will

When an emotional reaction starts inside you, not taking the bait and falling into the trap may require all the willpower you have. This Toltec exercise is designed to not only strengthen your will but also calm your mind in the process.

Find a chair with a straight back where you can sit with your knees at a ninety-degree angle. Choose a safe place where you will not be disturbed, and set a timer for five minutes.

Close your eyes. Focus on your breath. Do not move for those five minutes—not even to scratch your nose or to shift into a more comfortable position. If you move, restart the timer. Do not give in to the temptation to say yes to moving any part of your body.

The point of this exercise is to see how strong your will is by keeping your body still. As you are able to reach that time, increase that time if you would like, working your way up to fifteen or even thirty minutes. But before increasing the time, consider adding this element to the exercise.

Repeat all of the previous steps, but as you sit, imagine yourself alone on a beach, with nothing but the sand, the water, and the sun. Now it's time to run. Imagine yourself running, feeling the sand, the water, and the cool beach air. As your mind fills with this image, you may find yourself wanting to also move your body. Choose to keep it still without pulling yourself out of your exercise. If you get hooked by a chain of thought that takes you away from the beach, or if you move any part of your body, restart the timer and begin again, and again until you can go the full five or fifteen minutes continuously. As you will likely find, strengthening the will of your mind is more difficult than the will of your body.

◇◇

Both of these exercises can help strengthen your will so you can make a conscious choice in situations where you would previously have reacted emotionally. In the next chapter we will take a closer look at all the choices you make, so you can determine if they are a result of your free will or a habit formed by your domestication and attachments.

Chapter Six

Breaking the Cycle of
the Automatic

WHEN EUROPEANS FIRST encountered the Native American tribes of the North American plains, they were baffled by a small number of tribe members who acted opposite of the rest of the tribe. These tribe members would ride into battle backward, say "goodbye" when someone said "hello," and constantly do or say things that were the reverse of the normal customs. Unable to see through the fog, these Europeans found these warriors amusing and labeled them "clown soldiers."

But what these Europeans failed to realize is that these warriors weren't undertaking these actions to entertain anyone. Instead, they served a very special, even shamanic, role in the tribe. Modern scholars appropriately refer to them as "contrary warriors" rather than clowns, and as I look back on the role of these warriors, it is clear to me that they understood that without awareness, repetitive actions would limit the mind's ability to perceive all available options. Because these warriors made it a practice to respond to situations in an opposite manner, they constantly challenged the conventional thinking of the tribe, provoking them to examine their agreements and look at all options and possibilities. This is what I want for you.

If you watch yourself and others in the Dream of the Planet, you'll find that you, and most others, make multiple decisions every day without giving consideration to all the available options, and this practice seems normal to most everyone. For example, the route that you take to work every day, or the hand you hold your toothbrush in are automatic decisions. They are routine, the outcome is presumed to be known, and if you are like most people, you make these decisions without giving them much thought. Consequently, it is easy to go through your day without considering the possibilities, or even being *aware* that there are other possibilities—until there's a detour because of construction, or you sprain your wrist and have to brush your teeth with the other hand.

While making decisions automatically may seem acceptable with little things, if you aren't careful you can slowly begin to live your life on autopilot, and this will begin to spill over into other more significant areas as well. In other words, when you have developed the habit of making automatic decisions with all the little choices, it can become more difficult to stop and reflect on the larger choices when they are presented to you—especially when your domestication and attachments are trying to control you. In the Toltec tradition, we call this living in the cycle of the automatic.

To be sure, there is a place for automatic decisions, like those that help the body in times of physical duress. For instance, let's say you are hiking on a mountain cliff and your foot slips. Your body and mind instinctively come together to help you grab the ledge prior to plunging to your death. We can all agree that this is a very helpful automatic decision; it's a natural physical response. But compare that scenario to these: let's say an attractive person walks into the room and your first thought is, "They would never be interested in someone like me, I won't even try," or when you see a job opening and say to yourself, "I won't apply for that position because they wouldn't hire someone like me." In these situations, you can see where your domestication and attachments have limited your actions in a way that is inconsistent with what you really want.

Not approaching someone you would like to meet or not applying for a position you aspire to have is not the same as when our body acts instinctually, as the former are learned behaviors, rooted in past domestication of "not being good enough." If left unchecked, attachment to this idea will control you to the point that any choice you think you have is an illusion. A Master of Self cultivates the practice of awareness, and in so doing is conscious of the choices he or she makes so that they are reflective of his or her Authentic Self.

Only when we have cultivated the practice of awareness can we know if we are making choices based on what we really want, or if we are making choices based on our domestication and attachments. If we are lost in the fog, the idea that we even have a choice is a self-projected illusion. Without identifying and breaking the chains of our past, we don't have the free will to take any new actions. Awareness is the key to understanding where your domestication and attachments have made the idea that you have a choice an illusion.

Although I have used the word *awareness* many times in this book already, let's take a moment to examine its meaning more closely. Awareness is the process of focusing your attention on your body, your mind, and your surroundings in the present moment. Awareness is a unique practice, because in addition to paying attention to what is happening in the external world, you also watch what is happening inside your mind as well, noticing which thoughts arise and tracing their origins. The practice of awareness is a cornerstone of the Mastery of Self, as it is the primary way you learn about yourself: your likes, your dislikes, you domestication, and your attachments. Awareness is a conscious communion with yourself and the environment that surrounds you.

Another important benefit of being aware of your thoughts and watching them arise and subside is that it allows you to realize a truth we discussed in a previous chapter: You are not your thoughts. Your thoughts are simply narrators. Who you are is the aware energy that makes these thoughts possible. There is a beautiful passage in the Kena Upanishad, an ancient Indian text, that points to the nature of awareness and the Authentic Self quite beautifully:

> *Not that which the eye can see, but that whereby the eye can see . . .*
>
> *Not that which the ear can hear, but that whereby the ear can hear . . .*

Not that which can be spoken with words, but that whereby words can be spoken . . .

Not that which the mind can think, but that whereby the mind can think . . .

By learning about yourself through the practice of awareness, you are able to make choices according to your true preferences rather than any past domestications and attachments, and this gives you the freedom to exercise your will in the best way to evolve your Personal Dream and the Dream of the Planet.

Without awareness, your domestication and attachments will corner you into taking actions that conform to the belief systems they have built. This is not free will, as you have given up your personal freedom in order to maintain ideas that were planted in you long ago. When trapped in the cycle of the automatic, you are by definition acting without awareness. You have traded in who you really are for who you think you should be. By living your life on autopilot in this way, without awareness of the possibilities that exist anew in every moment, you end up in the same situations over and over again, making the same choices, and then wonder why nothing ever changes.

Other Manifestations of the
Cycle of the Automatic

Think about the people you encounter on a regular basis. Do you really see them, each and every time, as they are in the present moment? Or do you automatically assume you know the person, and as a result only see the image of them in your mind? Without awareness, your mind makes certain assumptions based on your past experience with the person. Consequently, you aren't seeing who they are today, but rather projecting an identity on them that's outdated and based on your shared past. In this way, someone close to you may be changing or trying to change, but you can't see it because you are attached to the previous image of them in your mind.

This doesn't mean that you shouldn't take into consideration your past experience with someone when making decisions in the present; but when you are aware, you can see that we are all changing, all the time. The person who is standing in front of you now is not the same as the person you saw yesterday. The difference can be subtle or great, but it is certainly there.

Another common misunderstanding occurs when you replace one automatic response with its opposite, and confuse that with a conscious choice. I see this often in people trying to break the beliefs of their childhood. When you disagree strongly with an idea that was forced on you as a child, you may rebel completely and do the opposite. Even though your intentions may be noble, doing the opposite simply for the sake of being totally different isn't free will, as both of these actions are part of the cycle of the automatic. You aren't taking the time to make peace with your past, look at all the available options, and determine if there is another option you prefer. You are simply rejecting someone else's idea of how to live your life and going to the furthest extreme against it. You are still giving power to your domestication, but this time in reverse, letting the opposite choice create an identity for you.

Choosing the opposite for the sake of the opposite is often dictated by fear, and any choice that is dictated by fear is not a free choice, no matter how well intentioned it may be. Once you have reviewed all available options, you may still choose to take the opposite course, but the difference is that now it's a conscious choice, made with awareness, rather than a reactionary backlash, and your actions are governed by self-love rather than fear.

Instead of being tied to an automatic decision or its opposite, awareness allows you to be conscious of all the possibilities that are available. You are aware not only of any domestication that is trying to control your choices, but also your reaction to that domestication. With the awareness of both, you are free to choose what makes you happy in the present.

The simple act of pausing before making a decision or taking an action, thinking about what you really want in a situation versus what may be an automatic choice, is the first step in breaking the cycle of the automatic. If you simply take a moment to be in the present and ask yourself, What do I really want right now? the answer, in some cases, may surprise you.

As you get better at practicing awareness, you learn more about your true preferences, and you build self-confidence in your own will. Conversely, as you become more aware of your current domestications and attachments, you will see where they have led you to make automatic decisions and judgments in your daily life. This is the first step to reclaiming your will and your freedom of choice, as the more you practice awareness the less automatic your choices and judgments will be.

Practice Makes the Master

Consciously making different choices can be scary. You're leaving your tried-and-true safe zone and entering into the unknown. Being a Master of Self does not mean that you may not be afraid when you make a new choice—you absolutely may be—especially when your choice pushes the limits you had previously set for yourself and thereby moves you into a new place. But it's only in the realm of the unknown that true transformation can happen, and making a choice you know you need to make to evolve despite any fear that arises is very different from allowing fear to dictate your choice. This is a self-evident truth that often escapes people.

As you begin to practice these tools, it's very likely that on occasion you will fall back into your old habits and make automatic decisions or choose something that isn't in alignment with your Authentic Self. Remember to be gentle with yourself in these moments, as when you begin to create a new Personal Dream there is a natural back-and-forth dance between automatic responses and awareness, between conditional love and unconditional love, between domestication and freedom. As you learn to spot and release your domestications and attachments, this awareness will more readily guide your decisions. Awareness is the tool to focus your intent and break the cycle of the automatic, and regular practice of this is what will make you a master.

Contrary Warrior Practice

For the next few days, experiment with doing small things in a different way than you normally do. For instance, if you normally brush your teeth with your left hand, try it with your right. Put the opposite shoe on first, drive a different route to work, sit in a different spot on the subway, etc.

While this may seem simple, diligently performing this exercise will help you in three ways. First, by becoming conscious of all the little choices you have throughout the day and by taking a path that is contrary to your usual choice, you will train your mind to observe what is happening in the present moment, rather than wander about as it usually does when it deems a choice is "unimportant." Second, by making different choices with the little things (some of which you may end up preferring over your normal choice), you prepare yourself to answer the question, What do I really want now? when the larger choices arise. Third, by making different choices with the little things in your life and discovering the variety of possibilities, you step into the unknown, or the only place where true transformation can occur.

Developing Your Awareness Skills

There are many things happening in and around you all the time, but you aren't aware of a lot of them because, like many people, you are lost in the stories your narrators are spinning rather than being present in the moment. This is nothing to beat yourself up about; it's simply the predominate condition that currently exists in the Dream of the Planet.

In this exercise, you'll begin to develop your awareness skills by observation. You will need a timer or stopwatch for this exercise, as you will want to do this exercise for two to three minutes at first, gradually working your way up to fifteen to twenty minutes.

Read the steps outlined in the paragraphs below one or two times, start the timer, and then perform the steps in the exercise from memory, based on what you read. Don't worry if you can't remember all the steps, you will get better each time you do the exercise.

1. To begin, sit comfortably in a quiet room. Turn off the TV, radio, or any other

device designed to hook your attention. Start your timer, and close your eyes.

2. Next, consciously bring your attention to the present moment. You do this first of all by acknowledging to yourself that for the next couple of minutes you don't need to think about the future or the past. The mind is often resistant to this idea initially, as it loves to spend its time in the past and future.

3. As you sit quietly in the present moment, bring your awareness to your ears and what is happening outside of you. Notice what sounds you hear, such as the hum of the refrigerator, the ticking of a clock, birds chirping in the distance, and the sound of your own breath. These are the sounds that the mind usually misses, as the narrators of the mind deem them "unimportant." If you listen deeply, you can also hear the silence that exists right behind these sounds.

4. Sitting quietly in the present moment, listening to what is going on around you, now turn your attention to within. Feel your body in all areas, moving outside

of your head where attention normally resides, and scanning your body all the way down to your toes. You are so much more than just your mind. Notice any areas of tightness, heaviness, or discomfort. Bring your attention to your breath. As humans, we take over twenty thousand breaths a day, but on many days we don't notice even one of them. Next, as you breathe in, direct your breath to any areas of tightness, heaviness, or discomfort in your body, and imagine that as you breathe out the breath washes away those negative feelings. Sit in this present awareness, eyes closed, surrendering the past and future, listening to your outer world and feeling your body in its entirety.

5. Throughout this process, notice what thoughts arise while you sit. Don't try to fight or control any thoughts, but when you notice you have gotten caught up in a thought chain, simply bring your attention back to the present moment, listen to the external world, and feel the entirety of your body and breath. When the timer beeps,

open your eyes and carry this experience of
present moment awareness into the world.

◇◇◇

After the exercise is over, make a mental list of the thoughts that arose. What was the predominate category? The thoughts that were most common are indicators of the things that are important to you as a person, and likely include areas in which you wear masks as you engage the world. We will explore the concept of masks, and the proper way to use them, in the next chapter.

Chapter Seven

Multiple Masks

HAVE YOU EVER NOTICED that as you engage the Dream of the Planet and the beautiful beings who share your Dream, you often project an image, or an identity, of how you want other people to see you in the world? This is a normal part of our existence, and playing a role in this way can actually be a helpful tool as you navigate the world, because doing so makes it easier for you to relate to others and vice versa. It's also probable that each of these identities or roles that you project is altered slightly to fit a specific situation or person. For instance, the image you project while you are visiting your grandparents is likely very different than the one you have when you're out with your closest friends.

In our Toltec tradition, we say that in all of these interactions it's as if we've borrowed a mask for a moment, or a temporary identity, so that we can engage with each other in a particular way. Wearing a mask is how people define and identify with others based on shared knowledge, roles, or experience. While the mask is a symbol that allows us to understand one another, it is ultimately just a symbol whose definition is subject to our agreement.

For instance, the masks I wear include husband, father, writer, teacher, shaman, runner, and soccer fan. Other examples of masks include how we relate to one another on specific topics of interest. If we talk about art, or yoga, or history, or any other subject we have in common, we begin to understand each other and see each other through the lens of our shared interest, as fostering relationships with others who share our passions allows us to shape our words and their meaning. When we engage each other, we stimulate each other's intellectual and emotional understanding, and interactions such as these allow us to co-create the Dream of the Planet.

As a Master of Self, I love to engage the Dream of the Planet and can use multiple masks to help relate to others and co-create more effectively, but deep down I know that none of these masks are the real me. A mask is just knowledge formed by the agreements we use to interact with life, with people. A mask is an identity. I choose to wear a mask for the benefit of navigating the Dream, but none can ever encompass my life force, my Authentic Self. When we are domesticated, the mask hides who we are and we believe that who we are is the mask; but when you have let go of your domestication, a mask doesn't hide, nor do we hide, who we are. It is just the agreements that our bond has created, and that has shaped the way we see each other.

This distinction, that you are not any of the masks that you wear, is vital, because when you believe that any role, identity, career, social status, or interest is who you really are, you have fallen into another trap, and suffering is right around the corner. That's because these roles and identities only exist in the Dream of the Planet, and like everything else in the Dream, they are subject to decay and death. Because of this, a Master of Self wears any mask with the full awareness that it's only a mask, a temporary identity to serve a function, and readily discards the mask when it is no longer needed.

For example, my wife may need me to be a supportive husband when she has a rough day, and I willingly offer her affection and security. At different times my children may need me to be a teacher, a friend, a playmate, and, yes, sometimes even a disciplinarian. I am aware that these are masks that I chose to take on, and because of this I can shed them the moment they are no longer needed. They do not become a permanent identity, and I do not try to fit into my loved ones' ideas of who I should be. I simply understand what they need from me at the moment and choose to act in a way that I feel helps them the most.

When you create an image of yourself as a worker, student, husband, musician, spiritual seeker, or any other role, and use that mask to relate to others, the moment you forget it's a mask your self-acceptance becomes tied to others' acceptance and applause as to how well you perform this role. If you don't meet the standards others have set for these roles, or the ones you have set for yourself, you reject yourself. This is another example of domestication and self-domestication in action, and it happens the moment you confuse any mask you are wearing with who you really are. Clinging too tightly to any mask only leads to suffering.

Another problem that occurs when you identify with a mask is that you will often try to keep that mask alive long after the need for it is gone. We see this in many manifestations in the Dream of the Planet, such as when parents attempt to manage the lives of their children long after they have grown up, or when someone continues to base his or her self-importance on who they were in the past, the proverbial "glory days." Both are common examples of what happens when someone attempts to hold on to a particular role when it's plain that the time for that role is over. Those who continue to prop up an illusion in this way are often unaware that they are doing so, but anytime you believe in something that is no longer true the result is always the same: you are lost in the fog once again.

This brings us to an important point: part of the Mastery of Self is being able to detach from any identity you have acquired in the Dream of the Planet. You, and everyone you know, have been domesticated into the idea that your name is so-and-so, that you are from this place or that, that you were born here and grew up over there, and that you like these things and that you don't like those things. These are what I call the first masks, and while they certainly represent truth at one level and serve a helpful function in the Dream of the Planet, all of these descriptive attributes are simply masks; they cannot encompass the aware energy, the Authentic Self, that you are.

I refer to them as the first masks because you acquired them in childhood, and they were projected onto you through domestication. This is a normal part of growing up in the Dream of the Planet, and it is something that has been happening for a long, long time. These first masks started before you were born, as soon as your parents learned of your impending arrival. While these masks were then handed to you in childhood, you soon took them and made them your own, without realizing what you were doing. You did so because you noticed that everyone else was wearing one, and it was normal to do so in your society and culture. Some of you may have worn a mask you knew was false, forcing it on, in order to be accepted in your family. As time went on, you lost touch with your Authentic Self, which means that you forgot that the masks you wore were just masks, and you began to believe they were the truth.

This is how you became intoxicated at the party, lost in the smoke and fog. When you make the mistake of seeing yourself as this mask, then who you think you are, and what you think you are, becomes confused with the definition of a mask rather than the experience of the Authentic Self. To be in awareness of the Authentic Self is to experience oneself as the energy that gives life to your mind and body, the power that allowed you to create the mask in the first place. Now, as a Master of Self, you are awake, and sober to the truth of who you really are. You don't internalize the identity, or the story, that the mask symbolizes, and as a result you can pick them up and put them down as needed.

Shape-Shifting

In the Dream of the Planet, most people you encounter are intoxicated to some degree, and as a result they can't see through the smoke and fog. Consequently, they project onto you the image or identity they want to see rather than what is actually there. The identity they assign you is based on their own domestication, attachments, and agreements. As a Master of Self you recognize this, and it allows you to *respect the projection of others, especially when doing so is helpful*. This is shape-shifting.

Knowing that others project a mask onto you, even when you have decided to remove your masks, allows you to shape-shift with awareness and compassion to suit each situation. Seven billion people will see you in seven billion ways, and every one of those masks is a single person's understanding of who you are. Your awareness allows you to not believe any one of their projections, because you don't need a mask in order to experience who you are. But you still respect their perception of you. You choose to see each mask as a mirror that will reflect different aspects of you, which you can either learn from or not. A shape-shifter is formless because life is formless. Mind you, knowledge creates and gives us form; thus, a mask gives us form in the perception of another.

For instance, let's return to the example of the grandmother and the boy from earlier chapters. Imagine that the boy has grown up and realizes that his grandmother domesticated him into always finishing his meal even when he was no longer hungry. Now that he is awake, he knows that it's better for him and his body to stop eating when he is full, and he discards the notion of "it's a sin to not finish your food" as a tool of domestication.

That's all well and good—until he goes to his grandmother's house for Thanksgiving. As you can imagine, she still projects onto him the identity of her little boy along with the domestication that he needs to finish his food. Because he respects her, he likely won't choose to tell his grandmother, "I reject your domestication and I will not eat any more food than I want." Instead, he sees the love in her intention, and with awareness he can choose to wear a mask at Thanksgiving for her benefit and finish all the food on the plate she provides him. However, he may also choose to feed his remaining food to the dog under the table, or discard it when she isn't looking, or say to her gently, "No thank you, Grandma. The meal was delicious and I am quite full at the moment."

With all these responses he is choosing not to disturb her Personal Dream because he sees the relative insignificance of finishing his food versus not finishing his food, and he plays along for her benefit. Because he is at peace with his past, there is no need for rebellion, nor a need to domesticate her to see he is right; his self-respect is expressed through his actions. Even though he can't keep her from projecting a mask onto him, he is aware that it is his choice to put it on or not. As a result, he is now acting with awareness of his past domestication and the many possibilities that are available in the present moment without losing sight of his Authentic Self.

Of course, there are other, more serious, situations where you may choose to reject a mask that someone is trying to make you wear. For instance, I have a friend whose husband, soon after they married, made it clear he had a very specific set of ideas of what it meant for her to be a "good wife." In short, he wanted her to dress a certain way, to not associate with her old friends, and to defer to his judgment when they faced important decisions as a couple—all things that she rejected. To give in to those demands would not be shape-shifting, but rather rejecting her Authentic Self entirely to please someone else. In this case, my friend refused to wear the mask her husband was trying to force on her. She would not shape-shift for his benefit, because doing so would violate her personal truth. She could see that he was trying to domesticate her, and that his beliefs were based on the system of domestication he grew up in. She ultimately chose to speak her truth from the heart, and fortunately he listened and changed his pattern.

Seeing others through the eyes of unconditional love allows you to make the best decision in the moment as to whether or not to wear a mask, or to shape-shift in their perception. The most important thing is that you be aware when someone is projecting a mask onto you, because then you can make a conscious choice as to what action you will take in each situation.

Projecting a Mask onto Others

While being aware of the masks others project onto you is critical, it's equally important to be conscious of when you are projecting masks onto others. When you project identities or roles onto others, you create a set of expectations for their behavior, and now the fog of conditional love has crept back in to cloud your vision. Through the projection of this mask you create an identity for this person in your mind, and then you judge him or her for not playing the part the way you want. If you are unaware, you can do this with your parents, children, friends, coworkers, or anyone, really.

Sometimes the projection can be subtle. This often happens when you assume that because someone feels or behaves in a particular way in one area of life, you think you know how they will feel or behave in another, often entirely unrelated, situation. Spotting and releasing instances like these are what makes you a Master of Self.

For example, I know a woman who I'll call Lisa who recently completed chemotherapy for breast cancer. In the eighteen months she dealt with the disease, not only did she fulfill her role as a mother of young children, but she also completed six marathons. She is a mother. She is a marathoner. She is a survivor. As I watch Lisa's interactions with other people, I notice that many of them project the mask they want to see on her. They set expectations based on how they think she should behave. Many of them only see her as a survivor and expect her to wear that badge with pride. When she does not live up to their standards of how a breast cancer survivor "should" act, they are offended. Why didn't she wear a pink ribbon during October? Why doesn't she raise funds for a breast cancer charity during all of her races? When those same people find out that Lisa is also a hunter, they often cannot assimilate their projections of the role of mother, marathoner, and breast cancer survivor with that of a hunter. How can someone so compassionate kill and eat animals?

At the same time, some people in the hunting community don't understand why Lisa runs all these marathons, practices meditation, and reads spiritual books. A third group of people, new runners, know nothing of her other masks and simply look to her for inspiration and support as they train for their first marathon. Each group projects a different mask, pigeonholing the entirety of her complex experience into one narrative that they have created. When she acts in a way that doesn't fit an idea they hold dear, it can trigger a strong emotional reaction. This has even led to some people trying to discredit or embarrass Lisa, because they took her actions personally and felt angry or hurt by them. Since their conditions weren't met, they deemed her no longer worthy of their love. To my friend's credit, she does not let any single one of the masks she wears, nor the masks others try to force on her, define her.

Lisa is humbled that people look to her for inspiration as they battle cancer or train for marathons, and she shows compassion when dealing with the people who may not agree with her choices in other areas. She is living her own personal truth in a way that will benefit both her Personal Dream and the Dream of the Planet. People ask how she could keep running while undergoing chemotherapy, and her answer is simple: "I did the best I could in every moment, and I never let cancer define me."

Because my friend is aware, she can use the masks others project onto her to engage in a meaningful way without detracting from her Authentic Self. She shares her personal experiences with breast cancer not in an attempt to define herself, but because she wants to help others by passing on what she has learned. By temporarily taking on the persona of the mask of a cancer survivor without letting it define her, she can remove the mask when the interaction is over. In this way, she demonstrates that she is in control of her actions, a hallmark of a Master of Self.

In summary, one of the greatest temptations you will face as you navigate the Dream of the Planet is to believe that any mask you wear is real. This is true regardless of whether or not someone else projects the mask onto you, or if you've created the mask for yourself. For instance, if things are going well in your life and you are succeeding at work or accomplishing your goals, your ego may want to create and hold on to the identity of one who has "succeeded" or "accomplished." We will cover the traps associated with this in more detail in the next chapter. Conversely, when things don't go your way, the parasite may scream so loudly that you are tempted to pick up the mask of one who has failed, or isn't worthy.

It is in all these instances that your practice of awareness can bring you back to the truth: the real you, the Authentic Self, is so much more than any mask can portray. Anytime you forget this truth and think a mask is real, suffering and delusion aren't far away. A Master of Self sees the mask as a tool, and uses the tool effectively when it is helpful to do so. Because she doesn't internalize the identity associated with any mask, she is able to remove it easily and return to her Authentic Self when the time for the mask is over.

◇◇

Identifying Your Masks

The masks we wear allow us to understand each other intellectually, emotionally, and spiritually. Of all the masks people wear, the ones we have the most trouble detaching from are those associated with specific roles in the Dream of the Planet. These roles include things like being a parent, a child, a worker, a student, etc. Think of all the roles you play in life, and list them on a sheet of paper. The very act of writing them down can help you see them as roles rather than who you really are. Next, examine the list and answer the following questions: Are there any roles on this list that you would like to discard or change? What steps can you take to do so?

Who Am I?

In almost all spiritual traditions, one of the most important questions to ask yourself is this: who am I? In the Toltec tradition, we often answer with "the Authentic Self" because it is a symbol that comes as close as possible to describing the truth. But even this answer is incomplete, because the ultimate truth of who you are is bigger than can be expressed in words.

Now that you know none of the masks you wear or the roles you play are the real you, take a few minutes and turn your attention inside. Ask yourself, Who am I? and see if you can find the answer within . . . the one that cannot be expressed in words.

◇◇

As we conclude our chapter on masks, let us remember a core teaching introduced earlier in the book: the world around us is virtual; it is all a dream. And in my family's Toltec tradition, we absolutely insist on creating enjoyable experiences in the Dream. In other words, we like to have fun! Doing so often involves setting goals to create something beautiful or to accomplish something special, but as you will see in the next chapter on goal setting, it's important that we do so with awareness. Otherwise we can quickly turn our Personal Dream into a nightmare. Setting positive goals for ourselves will help us to engage meaningfully and lovingly with others and the planet, and create the kind of life we want.

Chapter Eight

Goal Setting

SETTING, WORKING TOWARD, and achieving your goals are another beautiful way to engage the Dream of the Planet. Doing so allows you to learn and experience new things, to reach outside your normal limits, and it can give you a positive feeling of accomplishment as you manifest your creative intent through the application of your will.

At the same time, the practice of setting and achieving your goals can also be a trap to pull you back into the fog. That's because in the current Dream of the Planet there is a widely held belief that the best way to achieve your goals is to whip, chide, or use some other form of self-deprecation to push yourself to get to where you want to go. As a result, many people feel that the best way to succeed at something is to employ the iconic drill sergeant character in your mind, which pushes you with negative self-talk to "be all you can be." Seen in this light, it's not surprising how many of us have been domesticated to the idea that this type of self-flagellation is the only, and even the most desirable, means of motivation to get what we want. This motivation creates an obsession for an end result so that we no longer feel the pain from the spur of our own rejection.

One common way this method is applied is in the area of body image. For example, if you look in the mirror and decide that you don't like the way you look in some capacity—perhaps you think you are overweight, out of shape, etc.—the parasite will seize this opportunity and speak loudly, judging your existing beautiful body as insufficient. From this place, if you set a goal to lose a certain number of pounds or change your appearance in some way, because you are doing so in agreement with the parasite's judgments, implicit in that agreement is the condition that you will only love and accept yourself when, and if, you obtain that goal. The process happens so quickly that without awareness you don't even realize you have fallen into a trap. Of course, this practice of setting goals through conditional love is not limited to body image. As soon as you have an attachment to the outcome of your efforts, you've subjected yourself to conditional love. This can happen in any area of your life.

The problems with this type of approach are numerous. First of all, anytime you use negative self-talk as a means to achieve your goals, you imply that you in your current state are not good enough. This invites the voice of the parasite to come in and take over your mind, this time under the auspice that it is only trying to "help" you. This is yet another example of how the parasite can be sneaky, interlacing its negative banter with a conditional reward. But as we have seen in previous chapters, the parasite's methods always come with adverse consequences.

Secondly, pushing yourself to achieve your goals through negative self-talk leaves little room for self-acceptance and self-love if you don't reach your goal, setting you up for more internal berating in the future. This is the reason why not achieving a goal can leave you feeling worse than before you started. Anytime you use the voice of the parasite to motivate you, any failure to reach that goal just gives the parasite more material with which to berate you. If this occurs on a regular basis, the result is that you will become less likely to set goals or even stop setting them altogether, because on a subconscious level you are actually fearful of what your parasite will tell you if you don't achieve your goal. Anytime you stop setting goals based on fear of failure, it's because the parasite has berated you so heavily in the past that you don't want to go through that experience again. You would rather not try than face the fear of failing and hearing the judgment of your parasite yet again.

In addition, anytime you judge yourself for not meeting a specific goal, you also open yourself to being judged by others because you have already implicitly agreed with the judgment. This is also how the great majority of people interact with themselves and others, imposing goals and expectations onto one another and subjugating themselves to judgment if the goal is not reached. This method of goal setting is one of the primary ways that the illusion of conditional love spreads throughout the Dream of the Planet. In this way, you have rejoined the drama of the party and reentered the cycle of domestication and self-domestication.

Admittedly, the reason that setting goals in this way is such an effective trap is that sometimes it seems to work. The voice of your inner judge can be a powerful motivator, and it uses the tools of guilt, shame, envy, and a host of other negative emotions to push you to action. But even when this negative self-talk does seem to work, the success is short-lived. That's because when a goal is obtained through employing your parasite as your motivator, no matter what you accomplish, the parasite is never satisfied for long and will always raise the bar, making any self-acceptance through accomplishment gained this way temporary at best. That's why we say in the Toltec tradition that if you are waiting to be loved and accepted in the future, then you are not loving and accepting yourself in the present.

By tying your self-love and self-acceptance to a goal, your happiness corresponds to its achievement. When you reach your goal, your self-esteem rises temporarily; when you don't, you think less of yourself. This is using goal setting as a tool for self-domestication, as you have chosen to conditionally love yourself based on the success or failure of your obtaining this goal. Now the expectation of what "should be" controls you. The process looks like this:

1. You decide that the person you are is not enough, so you set a goal to achieve something.

2. You implicitly make an agreement with yourself that you will only be worthy of your own love *if* the goal is obtained.

3. If you don't meet the goal, you judge yourself accordingly. If you do meet the goal, your inner judge raises the bar.

That is the trap that the Master of Self avoids, and the way to do so is by loving yourself unconditionally, seeing that you are already perfect in this moment and there is no goal you need to obtain to be worthy of your own love.

Finding the Origins and Seeing Its Manifestations

At some point in your childhood, you set a goal to get better at one thing or another. Maybe it was a subject at school, or a game on the playground, or an instrument or other activity. You soon realized that by training or practicing at it you did get better, because you focused your intent toward a possibility. This is a wonderful process, and it gave you the satisfaction of creating something in the Dream of the Planet.

But there also came a point in that process where you were introduced to the idea of using self-flagellation and self-deprecation as a means to achieve a goal. You were given the idea that you needed to browbeat yourself into achieving your goal, and that your results would be better if you did so. Can you remember when that occurred? For most people, this happened at such an early age it's impossible to pinpoint, but in hindsight this was that moment when performing an action for the sake of the action alone, because you enjoyed it, was no longer enough. Your self-worth and self-acceptance became tied to the outcome or achievement. Fear and consequence were brought into the mix, namely the fear that if you didn't achieve the goal, the consequence would be that you wouldn't be worthy of your own self-love or the love of others. The moment that fear entered the picture was also the moment that achieving a goal became a tool for domestication, and before long you took that fear and self-domesticated. Let's look at a simple example that many of us have experienced.

When you first learned to ride a bike, you likely did so because it was fun, it gave you a sense of accomplishment, and it allowed you to do something other kids were doing. You later went on to other things, and you probably didn't give much thought to cycling anymore. But for the sake of exploration, let's imagine for a moment that you became attached to the idea that "I must be the best bicycle rider," and "I am only worthy of my own acceptance and self-love if I am the best bicycle rider." Unless you happen to be a professional cyclist, this idea likely seems silly, doesn't it? You can see the absurdity of making your self-love and self-acceptance contingent upon your ability to ride a bike, yet so many people do this when it comes to achieving a goal with other things—a job, a hobby, one's body image, one's role in their family, or even advancement on a spiritual path. This is how something that began as a source of fun and excitement can later become a tool for self-domestication.

Self-domestication through goal setting can be very subtle, and spotting it in all its forms is what makes you a master. You may think of goal setting only with definable, everyday tasks, but the implications of this type of thinking go far beyond that. For instance, what goals do you think you need to achieve or obtain in order to be happy in life or to feel complete? Do you need to feel loved by a specific person? Do you need to make a certain amount of money? Do you need a certain amount of praise, recognition, or social standing in your community? Do you think you need to obtain some great spiritual realization? Do you need your body to look a certain way? All of these measuring sticks are subjective, and only have the meaning that you assign to them. But what they have in common is that if you make your happiness conditional on achieving any of them, you have also made them tools for self-domestication.

As a Master of Self, the way out is to remind yourself that you are perfect in this moment and you don't need to do or achieve anything in order to be complete. It's absolutely fine to want to accomplish things in the Dream of the Planet, to see what your strengths are and see what you are able to do; but as a Master of Self your priority is to love yourself unconditionally throughout the process of working toward any goal you have set for yourself.

Setting Goals with Unconditional Self-Love

This can be one of the most difficult habits to change, as most people have been domesticated so severely and so subtly to the idea that negative self-talk is necessary to achieve goals that they have never even considered another way—setting goals from a place of unconditional self-love. But doing so can radically change your Personal Dream and how you interact with others in the Dream of the Planet.

When you think about something you want to accomplish, or some goal you want to achieve, the first step is to remind yourself that this is something you want to do. You know that in truth, there is no place to go, nothing to do or achieve, because any seeking of perfection outside of yourself is actually a movement away from perfection. Furthermore, you remember that the world around you is a dream, and that you are simultaneously the creator and the created in this dream.

From this place of awareness and unconditional self-love, you acknowledge that in your Personal Dream there is something you want to create, change, or achieve. This is you playing in the dream for the sake of play alone. It is not an effort to fix yourself, or love yourself conditionally. Setting goals in this context is a beautiful and natural process, and the methodology you employ to making these goals emanates from the knowledge of your perfection. Now you are starting the goal-setting process from a place of unconditional self-love rather than fear, shame, or doubt. Any change you want to make or goal you want to achieve is undertaken because you really want to do it, not because of a feeling of inadequacy or not being enough. You aren't changing because of your past domestication or current attachment, but to instead enhance and evolve yourself within the dream with something you love to do.

A wonderful benefit of setting goals this way is that when you have unconditional self-love throughout the process, you'll find that a natural self-confidence grows within you as you move along the path toward your goal's achievement. This is a very different type of feeling when compared to pushing yourself from a state of fear, where you are striving to get better because you are afraid of failing. Striving to achieve from a place of fear or lack creates a Personal Dream clouded in negativity.

When your confidence comes from self-love, you find strength in the knowledge that you can perform to the best of your ability and you will enjoy the moment regardless of the outcome. Because your own self-love is not predicated on any particular outcome, it's actually this love for life that is the true source of motivation to give your best effort. As a result, you are now in control of each choice you make along the path. You are open to changing the goal if a change becomes necessary, and because you aren't judging yourself, when other people judge your progress or your abilities, you know that this is a reflection of their dream, not yours.

To be clear, this doesn't mean that all the goals you want to achieve will come easily; they actually may require a lot of hard work! The difference is that by setting goals from a place of unconditional self-love rather than fear and self-flagellation, you are more likely to create real and lasting change as well as enjoy yourself in the process of working toward your goal. To explain this further, I would like to share with you an example from my own life.

A few years ago, I looked at myself in the mirror and said, "Miguel, you are perfect. I love you exactly the way you are, and I want you to be healthier and enjoy life, so you are going back to running again."

In years past I had run quite regularly, but I had not done so in some time. I had always enjoyed running and it had never been that difficult, and I assumed I could reach my old potential again with ease. Consequently, I dusted off my old sneakers and went for a run. My goal was to run five miles, but I only made it about two-thirds of a mile before I had to stop. I could feel my heart pounding, and I was surprised by my heavy breathing.

For those of you who are reading carefully, one word in the last paragraph shows you the exact moment I started down a perilous path. I made an *assumption* that I could easily run five miles after taking such a long break, and of course there was no way I could simply pick up my old running shoes and achieve this goal. By making that assumption I placed an expectation on myself, I set a goal that wasn't achievable. When I stopped running after going less than a mile, self-judgment immediately filled my mind as the voice of the parasite yelled, "Miguel, you are such a lazy bum." Upon hearing this my awareness kicked back in and I realized the old ways of self-domestication were attempting to regain their foothold.

At that moment I had a choice: I could berate and judge myself, or I could remember that this was just my starting point, and that as a Master of Self I will love myself unconditionally through the process. "Be gentle with yourself, Miguel. This is where you are today, this is my truth at this moment."

My goal, with practice, was to be able to run five miles without stopping by the end of May. It was January.

So I began my running routine, and like any busy father and husband, there were many days that I had to miss my run, or not run as far as I had planned. But I didn't beat myself up for any of this, and I continued to love and encourage myself through the process. On some days it took every ounce of my willpower to go out for a run, but I am happy to report that before the end of April I'd met my goal. While I was happy when this occurred, my self-acceptance or self-love was not contingent upon it. It felt really good, so I continued to run. Two years later, I finished my second marathon, and I am currently training for my third. I have been evolving my craft with passion while still balancing all that life throws at me.

My point is this: when you use unconditional self-love as the starting point when setting any goal, you remain aware that perfection is not tied to the end result, but rather the reality of the present moment. You were perfect at the onset and you are perfect now; you are perfect throughout. You are aware the entire time that the end result won't define you. It is through the practice of awareness that you are able to see the perfection that exists in yourself, which also lets you see perfection in the world around you and in each being in it.

Grounding Practice and Mantra

When you first begin to break free from old habits and old ways of thinking, you will likely find that both domestication and self-love are present simultaneously. In other words, you may focus your intent on setting goals from a place of unconditional self-love, but you may still hear the voice of the parasite attempting to push you through negative self-talk as you do so. Many times simply the act of being aware of the parasite will silence it, but here is a practice to re-center you when the parasite persists.

As you work to achieve a goal that you have set for yourself and you hear the voice of the parasite attempting to berate or introduce doubt in your mind, the first step is to take a break from what you are doing and go inside. Bring your awareness to your breath, focusing on the life-giving process that moves air in and out of your body. Next, feel your feet planted firmly on the ground below you. With your mental perception, imagine how you are connected to everything in life through your breath and the ground beneath you. Scan your body from head to toe, as doing so takes you out of your head and reminds you of what it feels like to be in your body. You are so much more than the voice in your head. Next, remind yourself that you are performing this particular action because you want to. You are already perfect, and you surrender yourself to the outcome. Repeat the following statement over and over until your ally regains control of your mind:

I, _____, am perfect and complete right now, I love myself no matter what.

Visualization

In the Toltec tradition, we recognize that the mind is a powerful tool for helping you achieve your goals. Here is an exercise that can help you harness the power of your mind and focus your intent on creating what you want. Do this exercise daily, preferably in the morning, as you work toward a goal.

Find a quiet place to sit for a few minutes. Close your eyes and consciously send unconditional love to yourself. Feel gratitude for being alive in the present moment. Feel gratitude for your body and mind, for they are what allow you to experience the Dream of the Planet. Next, turn your thoughts to the goal that you are working toward. Envision yourself achieving this goal, and concentrate on the feelings of gratitude for having done so. The key here is to feel gratitude as if the goal has already been achieved, as doing so makes this experience real in your mind. After a few minutes of focusing your intent on gratitude for already having achieved your goal, bring your awareness back to the present moment. Open your eyes, and go out and enjoy the process of working toward your goal.

◇◇

Setting goals with awareness can be a helpful tool to create and co-create in the Dream of the Planet, and remembering to love yourself no matter the outcome is the key to enjoying yourself throughout the process. Of course, there will be times when another human being stands in the way of you achieving your goal. The question now becomes, how will you react then? That is the subject of our next chapter.

Chapter Nine

Comparison and Competition

As we come to the final lessons of this book, let us return for a moment to the soccer analogy. But this time, instead of being a fan who is watching the game with a varying degree of attachment to the outcome, imagine that you are one of the players on the field.

As a player, it's your goal to win the game, and you have a choice on what you will use to motivate you to reach that goal. If you are motivated by the voice of your parasite, you will revert to self-deprecation and self-flagellation, where the only means by which you will love and accept yourself is if you win. If you apply the steps outlined in the last chapter, you can love yourself unconditionally throughout the process, enjoying the game for the sake of playing it, regardless of the outcome.

But there is a big difference between setting a goal that involves only you (say, running five miles) versus a goal that involves other people (winning a soccer game). In the latter, you will have an opponent who stands in the way of you achieving your goal. This is a competition, and the question becomes, how will you view your opponent throughout the process? Will you love your opponent unconditionally? Can you view your opponent as another manifestation of the Authentic Self? Or will you demonize them, see them as an enemy who must be defeated at all costs? How will you act toward your opponent if you lose?

These questions are important because in our society life is often portrayed as a competition. If you look around, a prolific message that is communicated via movies, TV, books, and especially advertising in all its forms is that all of the things you want in life are in "limited supply," be that love, happiness, friendship, a job or career, beauty, money, or material possessions, and because of this limited supply you had better do everything in your power to acquire yours before someone else does. This idea, often referred to in economic terms as "scarcity," creates a not so subtle atmosphere of comparison and competition between you and many of the people you know.

This idea of scarcity, and the subsequent competitive mindset, is so prevalent that it's difficult to spot in all its forms. For instance, when you first meet someone, notice if you start to compare yourself to him or her based on the things that are important to you as an individual. Do you assess the other person's physical appearance in comparison to you? Do you estimate their material wealth, education level, or social standing in comparison to yours? Or perhaps you question whether the person is "more spiritual" than you are. The modes of comparison differ depending on what's important to you, but the act of comparing almost always leads to competition, even if the competition only resides in your mind. The old cliché about keeping up with the Joneses acknowledges this comparative and competitive mindset. It's a habit, and it takes awareness and effort to break free of it.

It's noteworthy that the first four letters of the word *scarcity* are also the first four letters of the word *scare*, because fear is exactly what the idea of scarcity provokes. Fearing that there isn't enough of whatever they want, people view others in the Dream of the Planet as competitors for a limited number of resources, be that love, happiness, money, etc., and they act accordingly. As you have learned, any action that is motivated by fear cannot also be motivated by unconditional love, and it ultimately leads to suffering in one form or another. When you accept the concept of scarcity without question, the result is that you believe someone else may get something that you need instead. This is a very difficult place from which to engage others in the Dream of the Planet, as doing so turns them into opponents rather than friends.

In the Toltec tradition, we understand that the idea of scarcity, as it is most often promulgated in the Dream of the Planet, is a myth. From an early age, you are domesticated into the false belief that scarcity exists, but the truth is, there is always enough of whatever you need in this moment. When you believe the myth of scarcity, the result is that you feel afraid, you see others as competition, and in this way you get lost in the fog again.

Note that I did not say there would always be enough of whatever you *want* in the moment, but rather what you *need*. That is a big difference. You may have many wants or preferences in the world that don't arrive when you'd like them to, but a Master of Self knows that life will always provide exactly what is *needed* in the moment. This is not just a theory; you can actually prove it to yourself right now.

Take a moment to think about your past and identify a couple of meaningful situations where at the time you did not get what you thought you wanted. For example, did you want a promotion or a new job but didn't get it? Did you want to have an intimate relationship with someone who ultimately didn't want the same? In each situation that you identify in your own life, what happened instead?

For example, I have a friend who experienced this truth in a profound way a few years ago. He and his wife were coming up on ten years of marriage when she announced that she wasn't in love with him anymore, and she filed for divorce. My friend was heartbroken. He begged, pleaded, and did everything in his power to convince his wife to stay in the marriage, all to no avail. When she left, he sank into a deep depression, and he was convinced that this divorce was the worst thing that could happen to him.

But then he started to work on himself. As a result, he began to look within and release the idea that he knew better than life. Slowly, he opened to the idea that this divorce, although not what he wanted, was instead what he needed. After a year or so of further work on himself he was able to move on from his past, to heal the wounds that were there even before his divorce, and he started dating again. Shortly thereafter, he met the love of his life, and they soon married and now have three beautiful children. What's especially remarkable about this story is that my friend's first wife did not want children, and although my friend did, he was willing to give up that dream in order to be with her. In hindsight, he is so grateful to his first wife for leaving him, as otherwise he would not have his precious children and the fulfilling relationship he now enjoys with his current wife.

As my friend's experience demonstrates, sometimes there needs to be a certain amount of distance between you and the event before you can see the truth of this teaching, but if you look closely at the situations in your past when you didn't get what you wanted, you'll likely find that you got exactly what you needed instead. Even when the end results of a situation don't demonstrate this as clearly as they did in my friend's case, a Master of Self finds the inner strength to embrace this principle with an open heart.

When you live your life from a mindset of trust rather than a place of fear, the result is that you stop trying to force or control the people and situations that are happening around you and instead surrender to whatever life brings. This doesn't mean you don't try to change things when it's within your power to do so, but as a Master of Self you are adept at identifying the situations that are beyond your control, and in those instances you trust and surrender to whatever the moment brings because you know you will receive exactly what you need. Because you no longer believe in the concept of scarcity, you know that the place for competition and opponents exist in games only, not in daily life. You no longer compare yourself to others, nor see them as competitors. You simply do your best, and your passion will be evident in your efforts. Success is the natural consequence of doing something you love to do.

Closely related to the concept of scarcity is an idea we have already discussed at length: the notion that somehow you are flawed, broken, unworthy, or, at best, simply "not enough." I bring it up again now because the ideas of scarcity and that you are "not enough" actually work hand in hand to keep you trapped in the fog. Think about it for a moment. If the person you are is flawed, broken, or not enough, then it is unlikely that you will be able to acquire the things that you need because they are supposedly in limited supply. The combination of these untruths creates an environment where conditional love thrives through the vehicles of comparison and competition, and the result is the fear that you will never be enough, and that you will never have enough.

The idea that you are not enough is an ancient one, as it has been postulated in myths and legends since the beginning of recorded history. (The story of the Garden of Eden and Original Sin are good examples.) I find it amazing how many people in the Dream of the Planet have been domesticated into believing that they have some sort of inherent internal deficiency, and it is this belief that the parasite uses to take over your mind.

Of all the false ideas that you have been domesticated to, the idea that you are not enough may be the most damaging, so let me be absolutely clear on this matter: You are more than enough. You are perfect and complete exactly as you are. You are not flawed, broken, damaged, or irredeemable. Much of the suffering you experience is self-inflicted, and it can be traced back to believing this untruth. This feeling of unworthiness is the primary reason you withhold unconditional love for yourself. The most effective thing you can do to bring about change in your life is to let this flawed idea go. Once this false belief is replaced with unconditional self-love and self-acceptance, the myth of scarcity crumbles, and comparison and competition with others ends in its wake.

Perfection is something that is completely free of flaws. But the thing is, we define what a flaw is with our agreement. There is no such thing as a flaw in the world, just in the agreements that we make in the Dream of the Planet, and that is an illusion. Thus, everything in life is perfect.

Comparison and Role Models

As children we all had role models, or people we looked up to and wanted to be like. In many cases our first role models were our parents or primary caregivers, and that gave way to siblings, teachers, sports figures, superheroes, and even friends. As we grew up, our role models often broadened to include artists, scholars, humanitarians, political leaders, or spiritual teachers. In all cases, we saw qualities in these people that we wanted in ourselves, and often endeavored to emulate them as a result. This is a wonderful way in which admirable qualities are passed from one Personal Dream to another.

And yet, like many other things we have discussed in this book, something that can be used in a positive way can also become a negative. In this case, you can begin to compare yourself to your role model, and use their positive example as a tool to chide or whip yourself for not being more like them. You create conditions on your self-love based on a desire to be like someone else.

For instance, let's say that one of your role models is Mother Teresa, the famous Roman Catholic nun from the twentieth century who moved from Europe to India at the age of eighteen, founded a religious order, and devoted the rest of her life to helping the sick and the poor. There are many reasons to admire and emulate this special woman: her acts of unconditional love, tolerance, charity, and selflessness, just to name a few. However, without awareness, you could also begin to use her example to judge yourself as inadequate, saying something like, "I'm not helping enough people," or "I am not as good of a person as Mother Teresa." The minute you do this, then instead of looking at the qualities she exhibits as inspirational, you have now started the unhealthy process of comparing yourself to her, and using that comparison as a reason to go against yourself. In this way, the parasite has slipped in the back door and regained control of your mind.

Think about the absurdity of this for a moment. This is the last thing that Mother Teresa, or any other truly positive role model, would want for you. When you catch yourself comparing your life to that of a role model and then admonishing yourself for not being more like them, that's your cue that the fog has crept back in and clouded your vision. Instead of comparing yourself to others and deciding that you are insufficient, use your role models' examples as motivation to bring the qualities you admire in them to fruition in your own everyday life.

In my own case, I have a good friend who is close to qualifying for the Boston Marathon, as he can run 26.2 miles in 3:30. I look up to him as a runner and as a great human being, but the moment I begin to compare myself to him and his results, I am once again domesticating myself with someone else's achievements, and forsaking myself in the process. Instead, I celebrate his success just as much as I celebrate my own. I ran a marathon in 5:57, and I celebrate the fact that I finished it. Instead of comparing my time with his time, I look within at all I have accomplished, of how much I enjoyed doing it all. This allows me to enjoy my own craft, to enjoy the opportunity I have to do something I love to do, and to evolve my skills with my passion. I will learn from my friend, and many other runners, and enjoy our camaraderie.

Another trap related to role models occurs when you mistakenly believe that a single role model or teacher has all of your answers. A situation like this can often occur on a spiritual path, especially when you first start to wake up and emerge from the smoke and fog. Admittedly, depending on the level of your prior domestication and attachment, it may *seem* like a role model or teacher *does* have all your answers, as you are just starting to find your own way. But as the initial bud of your awakening blossoms, you soon realize that in reality *you have all your own answers*, and any role models or teachers you engage with are only there to point you on the way back home to yourself.

This doesn't mean that you don't seek the help of others when the way gets difficult; we all need help from time to time. But the difference is that as a Master of Self you know that on the deepest level, everything you need is already inside you. With a perception of abundance rather than scarcity, you allow yourself to be inspired by the talents and successes of others.

As a Master of Self, you are forging your own path, creating your own journey to your own inner evolution. You are grateful for the lessons from your role models and teachers and you are inspired by their examples, but you don't compare yourself to any of them, nor do you want to be just like any of your role models, because you are completely content with the person that you are.

In the end, you understand that you are unique in your experience of life because no one else knows life from your perception but you. It is liberating to become aware that you only control your own will, and this knowledge allows you to enjoy everything you experience and do. The harmony and peace that the Toltec warrior felt in the opening paragraph of chapter one comes when you realize that there is no need to work so hard to be someone you think you should be, because you are already perfectly yourself. The *I am* is an experience of life, not a symbol or model that you have to attain. In this way, the inner war is over, again, and again, and again. As a Master of Self, peace reigns.

The following exercises will help you put the lessons from this chapter into practice.

◇◇◇

Mudita

In the Buddhist tradition there is a concept known as *mudita*, or sympathetic joy, which is the practice of having joy in the accomplishments, achievements, and good fortune of others. This virtue can be easy to cultivate when the others are members of your family or close friends, but it is more difficult once you move outside your inner circle.

For this exercise, think of a situation where someone else received something that you wanted for yourself. Perhaps this was a promotion at work, an award, a material object, etc. Once you have the situation and person in mind, repeat the following statement out loud three times.

"I am grateful that _____ received the good I wanted for myself."

How did it feel to speak those words out loud? If you are like most people, this can be a difficult practice to feel sincere about, especially at first. But consciously bringing the practice of mudita into your life can help you replace jealousy and envy with goodwill and unconditional love. Doing so will help you to see beyond the myth of scarcity. Other people are not your competitors; everyone gets exactly what they need in every moment, and this includes you.

Going forward, as you engage others in the Dream of the Planet, become aware of your internal reactions when you are in a situation where someone else receives something you wanted for yourself. Notice if your feel jealousy, envy, or fear, and use that as an opportunity to practice mudita.

Role Models

STEP 1

Think of the many role models you have had in your life and make a list of all the qualities you saw and admired in these people. List the qualities only on a sheet of paper, not the names of the people. Some examples might be: honesty, generosity, tolerance, skill, peacefulness, discernment, etc. Make the list before proceeding to step 2.

STEP 2

Recall what we discussed in chapter 5 about mirroring, where someone who gets under your skin usually possesses a quality you see in yourself that you don't like. Well, the opposite is also true. Look back at the list of your role models' qualities. Now write your name at the top of this list. You possess all of these qualities! Otherwise, you wouldn't have been able to recognize them in others. You may not have the skill of your role model in certain areas, but you have the ability and the potential to forge your own way if you choose to work toward that.

STEP 3

Knowing that you already possess these qualities that you admire in others, what qualities do you think others would admire in you? How do you think others perceive you? Does that match up with the list you made, or are they different? Let your inspiration lead you forward.

◇◇

My Wish for You

THROUGHOUT THIS BOOK, you have learned various ways to identify and release your domestications and attachments. You've learned how doing so can help silence the negative self-talk that produces suffering in your Personal Dream and replace it with unconditional self-love and self-acceptance. When you bring this spirit of unconditional love to your interactions with others in the Dream of the Planet, you see them through the eyes of compassion and you respect their choices even if they differ from yours. Through the power of forgiveness, you are able to move past the harm caused by others and see that they were doing the best they could at the time. In these ways, you are doing your part to create harmony in the Dream of the Planet.

You have also learned about the power of masks, the art of shape-shifting, and how you can shift for the benefit of another as long as it doesn't violate your personal truth. You are able to set goals that are consistent with what you really want, and you love yourself throughout the process of working to achieve them. In the end, you know that you are already perfect and complete, more than enough, and you will always receive exactly what you need in every moment. While you are grateful for the lessons you have learned from others, you now have the confidence to walk your own path because you know that everything you need is already inside of you.

Because you recognize the suffering that domestication and attachment cause in yourself and others, you no longer try to control those around you with anger, guilt, or sadness in order to force them to believe or act the way you think they should. You respect everyone's ability to make their own decisions, which means you don't project onto them a mask of who you think they should be. Because you accept yourself for who you are, you are now able to accept every other person for who they are. This is a dream that we are co-creating; we are learning from each other and respecting every person's individual perspective. No one is more important than anyone else. Engaging from this place of mutual respect for all beings makes it the best world possible.

In those rare moments when you do slide and fall into a trap, as a Master of Self you are able to regain your awareness and recover quickly. Rather than making things worse by lashing out, being defensive, or otherwise falling into chaos and joining the drama of the party, you now have the tools to regain your footing. Through the power of awareness, buoyed by unconditional self-love, you know that you are doing the best you can at every moment. You no longer need to distort the world around you to fit your perception. You know who you are, and as a result you can act and speak with complete confidence and without apology. Thus, your word becomes impeccable. Because you are engaging others with awareness and unconditional love, you have confidence that each action you take will be perfect in the moment. In all of these ways, you have learned how to become a Master of Self.

Forgiveness for the Dream of the Planet

When we think of an act of forgiveness, it is almost always in reference to people we know, or those who have affected us personally. However, there is another type of forgiveness that is often overlooked, and that is forgiveness for the suffering that occurs in the Dream of the Planet.

To understand this type of suffering, let's look more closely at the two components that make up the Dream of the Planet. First, there is the physical world of matter, with its oceans, continents, winds, and shifting climates, where change is constant with every action. This is the phenomenal realm, or the world that can be seen and felt. Second, there is the world of human agreements, and these agreements are what give meaning to the material world. This is the world that is created in our minds and is based on our perceptions. The world of agreements is unseen, even though what manifests from these agreements appears in the physical world. While the physical world appears to move on its own, the world of human agreements by definition requires our participation. Let's look at two important events to emphasize the difference.

The first happened on December 26, 2004, when a tsunami in the Indian Ocean killed thousands of people in an instant. It was a tragic loss of life, but it is understood as something that happened via the movement of the earth, without any human agreement. While the outcome is heartbreaking, there is no one to "blame" for an event like this.

Compare that to another event that occurred three years earlier, on September 11, 2001, in the United States. This also resulted in the catastrophic loss of human life, but the cause was dramatically different, as in that case the impetus was a human agreement. Tragically, many people lost their lives because one group felt that it needed to subjugate the world to its vision of virtue with violence. In this type of tragedy, a sense of "blame" is placed on the perpetrators.

While it's perfectly understandable to be saddened and enraged over events such as these, and some of you reading this may even have been personally affected by one or both of these examples, when that sadness overtakes us we lose our perspective in the dream, and debilitating grief, depression, and, in the latter example, a desire for revenge can set in. In either case, getting lost in the sadness can trigger us to take a negative attitude toward the world, saying or thinking things like, "there is no use trying to improve the world," or "the world is a terrible place."

If you take this route, the fog has crept back in, as you are now living in your imagination, filled with fear and despair, and the Dream of the Planet has become a nightmare. You are taking the events of the world personally and letting them define you and your thinking. You have forgotten that during these tragedies, many people stood up to help the victims and survivors. Communities came together to heal one another.

While it's completely normal that both of these tragedies would evoke sadness, there comes a time when we move past the loss and choose to forgive the world for these events. You do so because holding on to the negative emotions generated by these events keeps you from evolving. That does not mean you forget what happened; it means that you don't want events like these to cloud your awareness and keep you trapped in the fog, unable to see the beauty that is all around you and keep you from co-creating the Dream.

Furthermore, a Master of Self understands that those who commit acts of violence (including gang members, terrorists, abusers, manipulators, and others) are actually the most domesticated and attached people in the Dream of the Planet since they have lost their ability to see the humanity of another living being. They are blackout drunk at the party, blinded by their belief system. They are so completely controlled by ideas that they can no longer see the humanity of their brothers and sisters.

To be clear, forgiveness does not mean apathy. Forgiveness in this context means that in order to create a harmonious Dream of the Planet, you understand that you are only responsible for you. You choose to let go of the anger and hurt in order to bring peace to your Personal Dream, and in that way you actually help the Dream of the Planet, so that one day tragedies that occur as a result of human violence can be found only in history books.

For a Master of Self, peace comes with forgiveness, by letting go of any poison that you're holding on to. If you let that poison drown you, then you become part of the cycle that has brought suffering into this world. To forgive the Dream of the Planet for the darkness is to forgive any place of darkness within ourselves.

Even when others make a choice to construct the Dream of the Planet by creating a nightmare, you know how to end the nightmare within yourself. Every time you choose to forgive, you heal the infected wound that causes you to cower in fear and hide behind anger. Choosing to act from a place of love rather than fear will always bring harmony to the present moment, regardless of what is happening in the dream. Forgiveness is an act of love, so in times of global difficulty I will say to myself:

> *I choose to forgive, I choose to engage, I choose to take action, I choose to use my voice for healing, and I choose to express the power of my intent through unconditional love.*
>
> *I am a co-creator of the Dream of the Planet, and I choose to end the cycle of conditional love.*

I do this, and I am letting peace begin with me. This is the Mastery of Self in action, and this is my wish and hope for you.

Acknowledgments

I WANT TO FIRST honor the people who taught me unconditional love: my mother, Maria "Coco" Ruiz; my father, don Miguel Ruiz; my Mama Gaya Jenkins; my grandparents, Abuelita Sarita, Abuelita Leonarda, and Abuelito Luis; my brothers and sisters, Jose Luis, Leonardo, RK, Kimberly-Jean, Jennifer, and Jules; my children, Audrey and Alejandro; and my wife, Susan (Lovie). I love you with all of my heart.

I want to honor and thank Randy Davila, my publisher, editor, and ink brother. Thank you for giving me the opportunity once again to share my family's Toltec tradition through these books, and for helping my Hierophant family continue to spread love and the knowledge that allows us to heal from the wounds of conditional love. Thank you for everything Carnal, it is a pleasure to work with you in this way! Love you!

I want to honor and give my eternal gratitude to Kristie Macris, who helped me start my journey into writing by helping me write my first book and helped me in the creation of this one. You are my teacher of this beautiful craft, you helped me find my own voice, and you are my partner and most beloved friend. As you say, you are able to translate what I say because you know me so well. Here is to twenty-two years of friendship, and many more to come. *Te amo!*

I also want to honor my dearest friend and teaching sister, HeatherAsh Amara. (High five!) We have come a long way since we started teaching together and dreaming of one day writing books and collaborating to create our art. Here we are!!!! =-) Let's have some fun! Love you!

Muchas gracias a Dios, con todo mi Amor.

Así sea, así se haga, y así se hara.

About the Author

DON MIGUEL RUIZ JR. is a Nagual, a Toltec Master of Transformation. He is a direct descendant of the Toltecs of the Eagle Knight lineage and the son of don Miguel Ruiz. By combining the wisdom of his family's traditions with the knowledge gained from his own personal journey, he now helps others realize their own path to personal freedom. He is the author of *The Five Levels of Attachment* and *Living a Life of Awareness.*

Hierophant Publishing
8301 Broadway, Suite 219
San Antonio, TX 78209
888-800-4240

www.hierophantpublishing.com